OTTER CREEK

True Stories of People and Places

GENE KEITH

MAY 2015

All rights reserved-2015. This book may not be reproduced in any form in whole or in part without written permission from the publisher. For information please contact Gene at gk122532@gmail.com

Forward

You can believe them or not, but the stories you are about to read are true. Some of the names have been changed to protect the guilty, but the people and places are real.

Would you believe a grandmother over in Cedar Key would take a .22 pistol and shoot an orange off of her grand-children's heads? Grandma Katherine did, and we have pictures of that very gun.

Would you believe a man actually killed another man on Main Street in Otter Creek for owing him 35 cents?

What would you think of a pastor who taught young boys to water ski in the ditches along the highway behind a 1950 Pontiac going 60 mph?

Would you like to know what healthcare was like before Obama Care? You are going to learn how country folks removed warts, stopped bleeding, cured asthma, hernias, and more.

You will also learn how to cook swamp cabbage, fried cat squirrel, and crabs & gravy.

We hope that you will enjoy reading this book as much as we enjoyed writing it.

Contents

Dedication   9

Chapter 1
Where in the World is Otter Creek?   13

Chapter 2
A Stranger and my Wife in a Pickup Truck   21

Chapter 3
Getting Off to a Bad Start   25

Chapter 4
The Otter Creek Baptist Church   33

Chapter 5
It Doesn't Get Much Better Than This   41

Chapter 6
Healthcare before Obama Care   49

Chapter 7
Fishing and Skiing in the Ditches   57

Chapter 8
Everybody Went to Chiefland on Saturday   63

Chapter 9
Fishing in Levy County   65

Chapter 10 Hunting in Levy County	79
Chapter 11 Whatever happened to Old Cush?	95
Chapter 12 Murder on Main Street	101
Chapter 13 Moonshine Mary	105
Chapter 14 Pistol Packing Grandma	107
Chapter 15 A Country Baptism	115
Chapter 16 The Fastest Deputy in Levy County	119
Chapter 17 Junior Williams and the Lucky Ticket	121
Chapter 18 Norwood Ishee Day	125
Chapter 19 John and Imogene Yearty	127
Chapter 20 Dick Parnell, George Bird, & Old Rattler	129

Chapter 21
Mrs. Thelma and the Phelps' Store   135

Chapter 22
The Old Watson Place   141

Chapter 23
The Watson, Gore, and Berryhill Families   147

Chapter 24
The Yearty, Williams, and Walrath Families 151

Chapter 25
The Byrd Family   159

Chapter 26
The Meeks Family   163

Chapter 27
The Haldeman, Baker, & Bishop Families   167

Chapter 28
Henry Strong: Great Grandson of a Slave   171

Chapter 29
The Gulf Hammock Community Church   175

Chapter 30
Rosewood: What Hollywood Left Out   179

Chapter 31
A Redneck Wedding   181

Chapter 32
Bill's Otter Creek Memories   183
- The Smith Girls   185
- My .22 Magnum   189
- The Cotton Mouth   191
- Jungle Drums in the Night   195
- Momma! There's a Bear in the Yard   199
- The Day I Fought the Bear   203
- Sissy! Stop eating the Bait   207

Chapter 33
The Miracle on Main Street   213

Chapter 34
The Hurricane from Hell   223

Chapter 35
Salt Island - Salt Kettle Remains   249

Chapter 36
The Rest of the Story - 50 Years Later   259

Chapter 37
Other People Who Touched Our Lives   267

Chapter 38
Honorable Mention   289

Chapter 39
Redneck Recipes   295

About the Author   303

Other books by Gene Keith   307

Dedication

This book is dedicated to Mr. Dogan Cobb, the oldest man in Levy County. Dogan is now 104 years old, but in my opinion, he doesn't look a day older than 75.

My wife Tuelah and I went over to Bronson recently and had the privilege of sitting down with Dogan and his wife Delores. We enjoyed shelling peas and talking about the *good ole days* in Levy County.

Dogan was born in Gordan pasture, which is near Rocky Hammock and North of Ellzey, Florida.

He served as the Tax Assessor for Levy County for several years before he was drafted into the US Army. When he was drafted, the governor of Florida appointed his wife, Alice, to serve in his place.

Dogan completed his United States Army basic training and immediately was shipped overseas. He waded ashore with his unit at Normandy beach on June 10, 1944, just four days after "D Day" when the United States invaded Europe.

Upon receiving his discharge from the Army, he returned to his position as the Tax Assessor in Levy County until his retirement. He then served eight years for the First Federal Savings and Loan of Bronson, Florida.

Dogan has been a faithful follower of Jesus Christ for many years and is well known in most of the churches in the Harmony Baptist Association.

He was married to his first wife, Alice, for many years. They have three children: Sandra, Billy, and Mary. When she died, he married Delores and, at the time of this writing, they have been married 33 years.

It is such a privilege to sit down with Dogan and Delores. He has a wealth of information about people and places in Levy County. In our last conversation (June 2013)

Dogan also shared information about the Rosewood massacre that we had never heard, and it certainly didn't appear in the movie. We will share some of those facts in chapter 30 on Rosewood.

The Cobb family is special to my family for a number of reasons. When I became the pastor of the Otter Creek Baptist Church back in 1954, Dogan's mother, Mrs. Missouri Cobb, was our Sunday School Superintendent.

I was a young pastor, still in college, and I didn't know much about Sunday school or leading a church.

Mrs. Cobb and Mrs. Anna West took this young preacher under their arms and helped me to become a successful pastor. I've also known Dogan's kids all of their lives and their families are very special to us. God Bless you, Dogan, for your faithfulness.

Chapter 1

Where in the World is Otter Creek?

Many of you have probably never heard of Otter Creek, Florida. Don't feel bad. Before I moved there in 1954, all I knew about Otter Creek was, that's where we turned right off of US 19 when we drove north from our home in

Tarpon Springs to visit my Grandmother Campbell in Gainesville.

Years ago, Otter Creek was one of the five small communities which at one time existed between Bronson and Cedar Key along the old railroad lines that ran from Fernandina on the east coast to Cedar Key on the west coast. Most folks have heard of Rosewood, because of the Rosewood massacre, but few folks remember the other small communities like Wiley, Sumner, Ellzey, and Gulf Hammock.

Gulf Hammock, Rosewood, and Otter Creek still remain, although most of the other small communities are gone now. When the last of the hardwood had been harvested from along the coastal hammock and the turpentine industry went under, most of those tiny communities eventually died out and the people had to move on to find work.

Perhaps Otter Creek remains because it was located at the cross-roads of US 19 and SR 24. US 19 runs north and south along the west coast of Florida and SR 24 connects Gainesville with Cedar Key.

By the time we moved to Otter Creek in 1954, most of the big timber had been cut from the coastal areas and there was nothing left of the once lucrative logging industry but the "tram roads" where the old railroad tracks used to run. There was so much timber in Gulf Hammock, in the olden days, it took a train to bring the huge hard-wood logs out of the hammock and up to the saw mill.

Old Post Office - Otter Creek

Hospital, Doctor, and Nurse - Gulf Hammock

Old Hotel – Gulf Hammock

Old Sawmill – Gulf Hammock

When we moved to Otter Creek, parts of the old sawmill were still there, operated by a small crew, and so was the commissary, where locals could buy food, clothes, and other needs. I bought a pair of blue suede shoes from Mabel Tummins, who worked in that old commissary.

Mack Hodges Old Store

That's Bobby Frank Hodge's mother in the top right hand corner of this picture. We had not seen each other in years until recently when we saw her in the cancer center where I receive my chemo.

This store was a real landmark. We could turn off of US 19, drive west to the checking station and then turn south to Williams Landing. We could also turn here, drive down to the checking station, and then continue west into the Gulf Hammock management area.

This is also where the Wild Canoe Race ends each year.

Old Locomotive

All that is left now in Gulf Hammock is the old steam driven locomotive that pulled the wood from the hammock to the saw mill. It can still be seen at the little rest stop in Gulf Hammock on the west side of US 19, just north of the old Circle K building.

From the very first day we moved to Levy County we were made to feel "at home." Usually, newcomers to rural areas remain "outsiders" for years, but for some reason, we were accepted immediately and Levy County has been "home" to us ever since.

Two Suggestions

There are very few things we enjoy more than reminiscing about "the good ole days" back in Otter Creek. But before we go any further, I would like to make two suggestions that will help you if you decide to visit Otter Creek or anywhere else in Levy County.

Learn to speak proper English.

The first thing you need to do is to learn to speak proper English like we do in Otter Creek. The little community you are reading about is called **Otter** Creek on the map, but locals pronounce it *"**Order** Creek."* They pronounce *"Order"* in *the back of their throats.* If you learn to pronounce words correctly, the way the locals do, it will help you if you ever happen to pass through Levy County someday or actually stop in at Hershel's store at the cross roads in Otter Creek. The folks there will think you are a local person and not a *Yankee* or one of *"that bunch from Tampa."*

Don't Criticize Anybody

The second thing we suggest is that you not criticize anybody in Levy County. Our children and grandchildren have married into so many Levy County families, you may run the risk of talking about my kinfolks.

Now, with these two things in mind, try to sit back and let me tell you about life in Otter Creek and Levy county, Florida

Chapter 2

A Stranger and my Wife in a Pickup Truck

Tuelah and I moved to Otter Creek from our first church, the Taft Baptist Church, just south of Orlando. I had accepted the call to that church while still a student at Stetson University, and spent less than one year there.

I was the first full-time pastor in Taft and it was really a challenge. They had no pastorium, and the salary was $15 per week. My mother sent us $10 per week to help with groceries, and my Aunt Emily Killen from Moultrie, Georgia, sent us $45 per month to pay our rent. We had two children at that time and after trying to commute to Stetson University three days every week, I finally had to drop out of school and go to work at the Correct Craft Boat Works in Pinecastle, Florida.

The End of the line

Before Disney moved to central Florida, Taft was the *end of the line*. Nobody ever went to Taft on purpose.

The circus spent the winter there. The train came through twice a day and Mrs. Dominie gave haircuts for 25 cents. There were also some strange looking characters with long white beards, who belonged to some religious group called "The House of David." The only important thing nearby was the Pinecastle Air force Base and their modern B-47s. This is now the municipal Airport for Orlando.

Correct Craft Boat Factory

One day, while I was at work at the Correct Craft Boat works in Pinecastle, Florida, a blue pickup full of cow hides pulled up there with my wife, Tuelah, sitting in the cab with a perfect stranger.

Deacon Buford Holmes

That stranger turned out to be Buford Holmes, who would become a life-long friend. Buford was a deacon in the Otter Creek Church and he informed me that someone had recommended me as a possible pastor. He asked me if we were interested and for some reason, I became interested. We agreed to come up for a week-end and preach a "trial sermon," which we did. For some reason known only to God, the people decided to call us.

We fell in love with Otter Creek, Levy County, and the people living there the very first day we arrived. That feeling has not changed in more than fifty years.

The folks in that church didn't realize how little I knew. I had been in the ministry less than one year and I didn't know a beginner from a primary.

All I knew was that I loved God and I was sure He had called me into the ministry and I believed with all of my heart that He would teach me what to do when the time came.

L.C. and Davida Williams

L.C. Williams and his wife, Davida, were sent by the Otter Creek Baptist Church, to move us to Otter Creek. They came with a large truck, owned by Sam Standridge, who was a Deacon in the church. They drove down to Taft, Florida and took all of our earthly possessions up to Otter Creek. Davida and L.C. became lifelong friends.

Years later, when my son, Bill, was the pastor in Otter Creek, Davida went to the altar during the invitation to give her heart to Jesus. She took him by the hand and said, "Brother Billy, I love you," and suddenly collapsed.

Pastor Bill caught her as she was going down, and gently placed her on the floor in front of the altar. She died right there.

To say there was excitement in Otter Creek that Sunday is an understatement.

Chapter 3

Getting Off to a Bad Start

We really got off to a bad start on our first day in Otter Creek. L.C. and Davida had already arrived and the truck had been unloaded and some ladies from the Otter Creek church were in the pastorium arranging our furniture.

The Bossy Old Lady

When I entered the pastorium the first person I met was a bossy older woman with blue hair. She was acting like she owned the place and started "bossing me around." I remarked to Tuelah after that saying, ***"That old blue headed woman and I are going to go round and round."***

That precious lady was Mrs. Anna West, and even though I didn't like her at first, she later became one of my dearest friends and supporters.

Mrs. Anna was actually acting like a mother to me and I had simply misjudged her. She was truly a blessing to us.

School Children on the Roof

Once we had our furniture in place, my next priority was to install our television antenna on the roof. We had just bought a new TV before moving from Taft and we were anxious to get it hooked up and working as soon as possible. It's difficult for a person to do this alone.

It just so happened that the pastorium was just across the street from the Otter Creek School. The timing also seemed perfect because school was letting out just as I was climbing on the roof. There were lots of kids standing in the yard watching me, so I enlisted several of them to climb up on the roof and help me.

As you know, it takes more than one person to keep the aluminum poles and wires from touching any electric wires. We were doing just fine until some parents and church members happened to drive by and see me and all of those kids on the roof. To say they were not pleased is an understatement.

Elwin Standridge

Incidentally, one of those young boys who helped me on the roof that day, was a little freckled face, barefooted boy with overhauls, named Elwin Standridge. We became lifelong friends.

Elwin's sister, Betty Jo, is presently a member of our church, The Countryside Baptist Church of Gainesville. So is her daughter, Nancy Scarborough, who has been the

Secretary to the Coaches of the Florida Gators since Steve Spurrier.

Don't Pee in the Rain Barrel

Our son, Billy, got off to a bad start as well. We were visiting Buford and Liza Holmes in their home pictured below. In those days, it was common to have a barrel to catch the rainwater. The Otter Creek well water was bad and the ladies would catch rain water to make ice tea and to wash their hair.

Our son Bill, who was four years old at that time, had to go to the rest room. He was out on the porch and that barrel looked like a good place to relieve himself.

Long story short! Mrs. Liza caught him peeing in her rain barrel and gave him his first spanking in Levy County. Precious memories.

Things Got Better

One of the first things we did after settling in was to find a good swimming hole for our kids to cool off in. We didn't even know a person who owned an AC in those days and the popular thing to do on summer days was to find a place to swim and cool off.

First Swimming Hole

Being new to Levy County, we had not discovered the many springs and swimming holes. I remembered crossing a bridge on our way from Bronson to Otter Creek, so we packed up our two kids and headed for the creek.

The water was dark, none of us were bitten by a snake, the kids had a great time, and we all went home refreshed. When we stopped at Mr. Buford and Mrs. Liza's after our swim, and told them we had been swimming at the Wacasassa Bridge, Mrs. Liza looked shocked and said:*"That's not a good place to swim. You should have gone to Wekiva."* We had never heard of Wekiva or any of the other beautiful springs in and around Levy County. When we found Wekiva, we felt like we had died and gone to heaven.

Grandchildren Enjoying Wekiva

Grady Phelps

Grady Phelps Jr., who was the Game Warden in that area, and whose wife, Hattie, was our Church Clerk, took me in his boat and introduced me to Wacasassa, Ten Mile, Double Barrel and points in between.

Buford Holmes

Buford Holmes, the deacon who had invited us to Otter Creek to start with, introduced me to Walker hounds and deer hunting. On more than one occasion, as I was getting ready to drive to the University of Florida to continue my education, Buford would drive up in his pick-up with Buckshot wagging his tail in the dog-box and the temptation would be too great. Too often I would change clothes and go deer hunting with Buford, rather than driving over to Gainesville and attending class at the University of Florida.

Dewitt and Murrell

When Dewitt and Murrell Watson introduced me to trout fishing on the flats, my college days came to an end. I finally dropped out of the University and began to pastor, hunt, and fish, full-time and enjoy the beautiful country.

Chapter 4

The Otter Creek Baptist Church

Second Full Time Pastor

In 1954 I Became the second full-time pastor of Otter Creek.

George Dunn had been the part-time pastor of both the Bronson and the Otter Creek churches, and he announced that he would go with which-ever church became full-time first. Bronson won.

Both the Baptist Church in Otter Creek and the Methodist Church in ElLey had been were part time churches. The same people attended both churches on their respective Sundays. Back then, nearly everybody got along. The Baptist loved the Methodist and even though we didn't understand the "Holy Rollers," we all loved them just the same

Vernon Clyatt

When Otter Creek finally became a full-time church, they called Vernon Clyatt to be their first pastor.

I followed Vernon and compared to Taft, Otter Creek was like moving up to the major leagues. Otter Creek had a pastorium and they also were able to pay a pastor a $50 salary *every week*. After living on $15 a week and providing our own home in Taft, coming to Otter Creek was like going to heaven.

Our "little" Preacher

The folks in the church in Otter Creek called me "their little preacher." I was only 22 years old and knew very little about leading a church.

I never tried to hide that fact so I did not resent it when Mrs. Anna West and Mrs. Missouri Cobb took this young pastor under their wings and began to teach him something about Sunday school, BTU, and the Harmony Baptist Association.

The folks at Otter Creek had no problem with me being a student pastor and transferring from Stetson University to the University of Florida. In fact, they actually encouraged it. Margaret Renfroe and Mrs. Marie Meeks both taught in the Otter Creek School and both of them had earned their degrees in education by commuting from Otter Creek to the U.F. in Gainesville every week for many years.

Family Started Growing

There must have been something in the water there, for soon after we moved there, we had three more of our six children. Sandy, Jimmy, and David were born while we were living in Otter Creek.

First Building Program

When we arrived in Otter Creek, there was no running water or rest-rooms in the church. I can't remember, at this point, where we went for those things, but we made plans to remedy this situation. Grady Phelps Jr. the local game warden, Austin Shivers and I borrowed some crude equipment and drilled a well between the church and Mrs. Cobb's house. We purchased a pump from Beauchamp's hardware in Chiefland, and behold, we had running water. Next we took up a collection and bought some lumber and built two restrooms on the West side of the building. We now had one for men and one for women with flush toilets and running water. We were so proud.

First Taste of Racism

That building program also introduced me to my first experience of racism in the church. You must remember that this took place back in the 1950s when the schools and churches were still segregated and Black families were not even allowed to use the restrooms or drink from the water fountains at the filling stations. It was really sad.

One of the new rooms we had built was designed to be used as a church nursery. I thought it would be a good idea to hire a colored lady to care for the nursery so our mothers could attend church.

We called a business meeting to make our plans and when I suggested that we hire a Black lady to supervise the nursery, one of our members who was seated on the second row stood up and said:

"I'll tell you what! The first N****er who walks in that door, I'm walking out." It broke my heart. I'm glad those days are behind us.

First Hospital Visit

Up until we moved to Otter Creek, I had made only one hospital visit in my life. Soon after moving to Otter Creek I learned that one of our members was dying in the VA hospital in Lake City. Being a little nervous was only part of the problem. The real problem was I didn't have enough gas to make it from Otter Creek to Lake City.

"Ole Pal" (W.S. Yearty)

I swallowed my pride and drove down to see "Ole Pal" Yearty, who was our church Treasurer. When I drove up, Ole Pal was out behind John Yearty's house plowing with his old mule. I asked him if I could get my paycheck early to buy some gas to visit our member who was dying in the hospital. He readily agreed and I was on my way to make my first official visit as their new pastor. The following Sunday the church gave me a raise.

First VBS Parade

On the brighter side, when the time came for our first Vacation Bible School, Tuelah got the bright idea that we should have a VBS parade.

We borrowed a jeep from Deacon Sam Standridge, built a frame with 2x4s and chicken wire. We bought all the Kleenex the Suwannee Store had in stock and made our first float.

On the day of the parade, Tom Gore the Constable, led the parade in his 37 Ford Coupe and the kids from the church followed behind right down main street, past the Suwannee and Smith's Store, on down to Miss Julia's store and wound up in front of Phelps' store at the intersection of Main street and SR 24. It was a huge success. I think everybody in the parade would have been in VBS anyway, but at least we followed the book.

First Baccalaureate Service

The senior class of Bronson High School would usually invite one of the local pastors to preach to the graduates on

Baccalaureate. This was undoubtedly the largest crowd we country preachers ever got to preach to, and we all took that responsibility seriously. We would usually buy a new suit of clothes for the occasion if we could afford it.

Pastors Respected

Back then people still respected men of God. The word "Parson" came from the word "Person." There was a time in American history which the pastor was the most respected person in the entire community. Things sure have changed now.

First Stolen Property

Our son, Bill was about three years old when we moved to Otter Creek. His favorite toy was a teddy bear and he took it with him everywhere he went. . Bill had wet the bed so often his teddy bear was "water logged" and smelled to high heaven. We nicknamed it "Stinking Teddy."

One Sunday morning, while in church, Teddy stunk so bad, Tuelah made Billy leave the teddy bear on the front porch.

In those days, dogs always slept on the porch of the church. That day, when Tuelah put *Stinking Teddy* out on the porch, a dog grabbed it and ran off with it and we never saw "Stinking Teddy" again.

Chapter 5

It Doesn't Get Much Better Than This

Most of the old timers we knew in Otter Creek have passed on now, but their memories are forever etched in my mind. I will share some of their stories in a moment, but first let me say that we are living in the end of an era. My grandchildren will never have the joy of knowing the America I grew up in and loved.

People who touched our Lives

In this book, I would love for you to get a glimpse of the Otter Creek I knew, with families like the Holmes, the Wests, the Renfroe's, the Standridge's, the Yearty's, the Phelp's, The William's, the Meek's, the Watson's, the Berryhill's, the Cobb's, the Parnell's, and many others.

Things were not perfect in those early days in Otter Creek, but a lot of things were much better then, than they are today. It saddens me to feel like those good old days are gone forever.

The Hammock

When we moved to Otter Creek in 1954, the hammock was full of deer, turkey, and wild hogs. Florida Crackers call those wild hogs "piney-woods-rooters" because of their long narrow snouts. Their long, skinny snouts reminded you of the hood on a Model-T Ford. Those hogs are naturally skinny but the hammock hogs were often fat after eating white-oak acorns in the hammock and fiddler crabs that swarmed over the mud flats on the marsh at low tide. You could go down to the marsh and kill a nice shoat just about any time. Florida Crackers would eat sows or boars. It didn't make any difference. A hog was a hog. They ate lot of fresh venison too.

Fast Food

Most Fast Food (venison and gator tail) was taken by fire hunting. Fire hunting is taking deer at night with a light. It's illegal but was popular back then.

Fire hunting got its name because of the way the old timers did it. They would tie a frying pan on a cypress pole and carry it over their shoulder. They would then place some *lite'rd knots* in the frying pan and light them on fire. Then they would ease through the woods shining eyes. When the deer would look at the light, their eyes would shine and the hunters would shoot them. This was by far the easiest way in the world to kill a deer. Over time they *near 'boutkilled 'em all.*

Years later, the Game Commission released some big-rack Wisconsin Bucks in the area. One family in Ellzey (their names are withheld to protect the guilty) killed all eight of those big bucks in just one night.

Safe Highways

We seldom heard of a car hitting a deer on the highway 'cause Bug W kept the highways safe. "Bug" and his friends would take lights and guns and patrol the highways at night. When they would see a deer feeding dangerously close to the highway, they would shoot a couple of times to scare it away. Usually they scared the deer *slap to death*. At least, the highways were safe for our families.

Lived off of the land

Back then we didn't have welfare, food stamps, SSI, and there was very little un-employment, but it didn't matter much because most folks could literally live off of the land.

Any able-bodied soul could cut *booger-wood*, grunt worms, pull moss, gather deer-tongue, raise hogs, kill gators, or make a little moon-shine. Somehow, most folks seemed to make out alright. There's plenty to eat in the woods and in the water if a fella's smart enough to catch it or kill it.

New Pastor in Steinhatchee

It's *kinda like* the time the Baptist church up in Steinhatchee called a new preacher. The chairman of the deacon body took the new pastor down to the Gulf. Pointing toward the flats the deacon said: "*Preacher! There's plenty a' groceries out there on them there flats. Just hep' yo-self!*"

No War on Poverty

We had never heard of any "war on poverty." We were all poor but it didn't seem to bother anybody. We got along just fine. We could buy groceries on credit at the Suwannee Store in Otter Creek and hardware at Beauchamp's in Chiefland.

If Beauchamp's didn't have it, Sears and Roebuck did, and they would deliver it to Otter Creek on a truck and let us pay for it "on time." If Beauchamp's or Sears didn't have it, we figured we didn't need it anyway, so we quit worrying about it.

The Schools

The schools were much better back then. Many of the same teachers who taught Sunday school on Sunday, taught Monday school on Monday. Students prayed and read the Bible daily.

Margaret Renfroe and Marie Meeks taught school in Otter Creek for years. Mrs. Marie taught more than 30 years. She also taught Sunday school in the United Methodist Church of Ellzey for 70 years.

Teachers were our role models and were respected throughout the county. Parents and teachers worked together. If a student treated a teacher disrespectfully in school, that student would be in deep trouble at home.

Parents supported teachers and nearly everybody turned out for school functions. Those same students are grown now and many have become community leaders and outstanding citizens. I am sure, that growing up in Levy County had a lot to do with the way they turned out.

"Pot and Grass"

There were no drug problems in Levy County back then. Oh, yes, we had "pot" and "grass" back then, but we didn't smoke it. Our boys mowed the "grass" on Saturdays and our mommas washed clothes in the "pots" on Monday.

In 1959, I was a chaperone for the senior class of Bronson High School. We went to New Orleans for the Senior trip that year and there was not one student in that entire class that even smoked tobacco, much less pot or grass. Things were different back then.

Sports

Everybody loved sports, but they didn't worship sports. I remember when Cedar Key and Bronson played 6-man football. They didn't need a bus. Their entire team could travel to an away game in one four-door car.

Number Four Bridge

There was, however, a problem if you beat Cedar Key on their home field. You would have to fight the boy's parents at the Number Four Bridge to get off of the island.

One of the biggest "events" to ever take place at the Number Four Bridge was when a coach (who is now a personal friend of mine) from Williston took his team, which included some Black players, to Cedar Key. They called this coach *"The long-hair, hippy radical, from Williston."*

The Williston team won and you can guess what happened. That's right. The Cedar Key parents had the highway blocked at the Number Four Bridge and somebody had to call the Florida Highway Patrol to help the Williston bus get across the bridge and begin their trip back to Williston.

The Environment

Back then we'd never heard of the ozone layer, global warming, or an environmentalist. Down in the quarters, the colored folks burnt tires in their yards at night to keep the *skeeters* away.

When we'd change the oil in our trucks we'd recycle it by letting it pour out on the ground and sink back in. That's where it came from in the first place and that's where *we figger* it should return. It was *sorta like* the words the preacher recites at a funeral: "Ashes to ashes, dust to dust."

Outhouses

A lot of folks still went to the bathroom in out-houses and used Sears and Roebuck catalogues for toilet paper. When the hole got full they would simply cover it up and move the house up a bit and start all over again.

Most out houses had shade trees nearby and it was quite restful to sit there and read the Sears catalogue and let nature take its course.

We had to watch out on Halloween night though, because the local boys would often move the outhouse back about five feet so we'd fall in the hole before we got there if anybody went to the bathroom at night.

Conservative Values

Values were different too. If a school teacher back then had even dared pass out condoms or talk about "alternate life styles," our parents would have run them across the county line before sundown. Back then, the parents who were elected to the School Board had some say-so as to what went on in their schools. That's the way things were back in the good ole days.

We Loved America

Back then, most folks we knew believed that America was the best place on earth to live and Levy County was the best place in America. I've never met a person who has lived in Otter Creek or Gulf Hammock who wouldn't return there to live if they could. We had everything we needed.

We Had it All

We had an elementary school (called OCS), a blinking light at the intersection of US 19 and SR 24, a US Post Office, and of course, the First Baptist Church.

We also had the Suwannee Store, the Smith Store, Miss Julia's Store and the Phelps' Store.

In addition to all of that we had three filling stations. There was John Moody's, Howard Williams', and Lawrence Lee's, and each one of them had a gas pump, a drink box, and a free air hose. What more *could a body* want?

The Atlantic Coastline Railroad ran north and south, parallel to US 19 once a day, and for excitement, we could drive down the intersection, sip on a cold drink and watch the train roll by. If we were real lucky we would even get to wave to the conductor. Wow! How exciting that was.

As we mentioned earlier, the woods were full of deer, hogs, wild turkey, and swamp cabbage. The creeks were full of fish. There were oysters at Cedar Key and clams off of Shell Mound.

On the Fourth of July, folks would drive from all over the county to picnic at the head of Wekiva Springs. Back then, you knew just about everybody in the County. Today, we may not know the new neighbors down the road who just moved up from South Florida. Times sure have changed.

Sunday Nights

After church on Sunday nights we would all go down to Lawrance Lee's Standard Station, buy an RC Cola and visit with friends. The talk would be about hunting, sports, politics, and what was going on in the county. Often there would be *twenty five to thirty head-a people* (*This is not misspelled. This is Otter Creek talk*) down there *a-sippin'* on *RC Colas* and passing the time away. We'd often wink at each other and say, "*It don't get much better than this.*"

Chapter 6

Healthcare before Obama Care

Nobody had ever heard of an HMO or Obama Care back then, but we didn't need either because we had the best health care in the world.

Aunt Minnie, the County Nurse would come on a regular basis, and if we took *bad sick* (local dialect), we could drive up to Chiefland and see the one armed doctor who had an office there.

I will tell you more about Aunt Minnie and the one arm doctor in a minute. But first, let me tell you about health care in Otter Creek.

Bleeding

If one of us got cut, we could go down to Mr. Mack's place down past the old checking station. Mr. Mack would recite some verse from the Old Testament and stop the bleeding.

Burns

If we got burned, we could go down the street that runs north in front of the Phelps' store and Tom Gore's wife could talk the fire out of a burn.

Remove Warts

If anyone had warts, they could do one of two things, depending on how serious a case they had. If it was just one or two warts, we could go down to the quarters where an old Black lady would buy the warts off of us for 10 cents each. Usually the warts would fall off in a few weeks if you didn't spend the money. If you spent the money the cure wouldn't work.

On more serious cases she would rub the warts with an old dish-rag and bury it. When the rag rotted the warts would fall off. But you had to be careful not to tell anybody 'cause if you told anybody, the warts wouldn't fall off.

Sore throat

If we got a sore throat, we would soak a sock in kerosene and tie it around your neck. In about two nights our throats would heal. The old timers believed that kerosene would heal just about anything. If our dogs took distemper we would *feed 'em* wasp nests.

Thrush mouth

If a baby took thrush-mouth, we'd go down to the quarters and find a "blue-gum" and pay him to blow into the *youngun's* mouth. Blue gums are just naturally lucky.

Their breath can cure thrush and they can just about always catch fish. The only real danger is, the old timers told us, that if they bite you, you will die.

Cure for Asthma

If somebody got asthma, we could take them down to the back side of the hammock, to a place they'd never been. We would have them back up to a sweet-gum tree with their eyes closed. Then we would take a copper nail and drive it into the tree just above their head. Then we'd take them by the hand and lead them away without looking back. If they looked back it wouldn't work. When the child grew taller than the nail in the tree, their asthma would be gone.

For some reason it worked a lot better if the person driving the nail into the sweet-gum had never seen his daddy. We were so blessed.

Little Virgil's Hernia

The late Mrs. Nita Stanley told us about a little boy up in Baker County named Virgil, who had a hernia. Virgil's folks saw no sense in taking Virgil all the way to Jacksonville for such minor surgery, because there were some old timers in McClenney who knew *a sure fire way* to cure a hernia without invasive surgery. That's what they did to Virgil.

The old timer's believed that you could cure a hernia by passing the child through a sweet-gum tree that had been split and chocked open. Nobody knew why it worked. They all just knew that it *did* work.

So, one morning, *bright'n early*, they bundled little Virgil up and took him down to the hammock where they found a sweet-gum tree that was about the right size.

The men took their axes and split the tree open about three feet, just big enough to pass little Virgil through it.

They cut a limb and made a chock and stuck it in the tree to hold the two sides of the tree apart while they passed the little *young'n* through the opening.

Then, they picked little Virgil up and *commenced to pass his little body through the opening* in the tree and that's when it happened.

While passing Virgil through the split in the tree, Virgil's knee hit the limb that was being used as a chock to keep the tree open, and when it did, the chock fell out and the two halves of the sweet-gum tree slammed together right on Virgil's tiny ankles. It broke both of Virgil's ankles!

It took quite a while for little Virgil's ankles to heal up for him to walk on them again, and Virgil told folks that his broken ankles hurt him a whole lot worse than his hernia did.

Hoot Owls

We also knew how to *make owls stop hoot'n*. Back then, for some reason, a lot-a-young'ns started frett'n when owls hooted at night. We all knew that when owls started hoot'n the night critters were crawl'n and the deer were beginning to feed. We also knew when a dog would howl at night, somebody *was fix'n to die.*

Well, a man named Thomas, who owned a fish camp on Orange Lake, taught me how to make the owls hush up.

He said: "Preacher! When you go to bed at night, hang your breeches on the bedpost with the pockets a-sticking out.

When the owls start hooting and the kids get to frettin', *jus git up, take both hands and twist them pants-pockets with all yur might.*

As quick as a flash, he said, "you'll choke that owl right down and he'll hush right up! *I seen it a heap o' times.*"

Aunt Minnie: The County Nurse

The late Aunt Minnie Radacky was the County Nurse and she lived over in the flat-woods near Williston. Minnie and her sister Thelma had grown up poor but somehow Minnie had managed to take nurse's training and get a job with the County.

Aunt Minnie drove a Ford car with a big trunk. Minnie's trunk was like a drug store. She carried worm medicine, purple stuff for ground itch, and all kinds of shots. Most of the kids would run and hide when they saw Aunt Minnie's Ford coming into Otter Creek. Some called her "the shot lady." Back in those days, some folks in Otter Creek had open wells and out-houses. Blow flies were bad and most dog puppies died of distemper.

Aunt Minnie

Purple Feet

Most of the children had worms of some sort, and almost all of the children had ground itch. When Aunt Minnie would pull up in front of Phelps' store, owned and operated by her sister Thelma, by then, a widow with six children, mommas would fetch their children from their hiding places and line them up for Aunt Minnie to examine. You could tell when Aunt Minnie had been to town. Every *young'n* in town would have purple feet.

By the way, most kids went barefoot to church and to school. In fact, Toad Curry was the first *young'n* in Otter Creek to have a pair of lace up shoes. His parents were so proud. What they didn't know was that Toad would leave home with his lace up shoes on, but when he got close to the Otter Creek school he would hide his shoes in the bushes so the kids wouldn't laugh at him. When school was out, Toad would get his shoes from the bushes, put them on, and wear them home.

Panic in the Otter Creek School

One day in Otter Creek Elementary School the silence was interrupted when a young child started crying, "*I smell the shot woman!*" "*I smell the shot woman!*" Aunt Minnie was nowhere to be seen. But someone down the hall had opened a bottle of rubbing alcohol and when the smell of *rubbin' alcohol* drifted down the hall and into the classroom, that poor child thought she had smelled Aunt Minnie.

Sissy's Miracle

Perhaps no one hated to see Aunt Minnie's Ford more than our daughter Thereasa, nicknamed "Sissy." Sissy hated shots with a passion and even though she was not a large child, it took four adults to hold her to give her a shot. We tried everything to calm her down but to no avail. We even tried to intimidate her by having Constable Tom Gore stand there with his .38 in his belt, looking important. That didn't impress Sissy at all. She still pitched a fit. When we'd hold her down and Aunt Minnie would come at her with that needle you could hear her *hollar* as far away as the Elzey Bridge on SR 24. Then one day we witnessed a miracle. One day Tuelah arranged for Sissy to get a "store bought" permanent wave down at Mrs. Ferrell's house, and it changed her life.

We never understood the connection. But for some reason, after getting her hair curled, Sissy no longer *cut the buck* when Aunt Minnie came to town. In fact, not only did we not have to hold her anymore, Sissy would walk to the head of the line and ask to be first. It's amazing what a hair-do will do for a woman.

Chapter 7

Fishing and Skiing in the Ditches

During the raining season, the woods would flood and the ditches would over-flow with water. When the ditches flooded, the boys would skip school and spend entire days fishing in them.

I remember standing at one culvert by Bug Watkin's house in Gulf Hammock, with a dip net, and filling a foot-tub with bream and war-mouth perch.

On one particular occasion, our son, Bill was home sick. I went down to the culvert in front of Bug's house, caught a mess of stump knockers and warmouth perch, took them home and turned them loose in the bathtub so Bill could see them and not miss out on the fun.

Water skiing in the Ditches

Before we ever began water skiing in the Wacasassa River behind boats, I taught a lot of the young boys in Otter Creek how to water ski by pulling them behind a 1950 Pontiac in the ditches on SR 24 just west of Ellzey.

We pulled them behind a Pontiac because none of us had a *kicker (that's what we used to call an outboard)* or a boat that would pull skis. Grady Phelps, the Game Warden, had a 15 HP Evinrude, but we didn't borrow that until later.

For some reason I could never get them over 60 mph behind my Pontiac before they fell off the skis and started skipping like a rock across a pond. We were extra cautious back then and trained the young boys to let go of the ski rope before they reached the culverts.

The Rivers Were Safe

When we finally "moved up" to skiing in the Wacasassa, the rivers were much safer back then than they are today because Grandpa Dewitt kept the gator population under control.

Back in those days a whole pack-of Walker hounds could run a deer across the Wacasassa River and down to the marsh without *gettin' et by a gator*. Have you ever seen a dog that had got gator caught? Gators eat the belly *slap out of a dog.* We didn't want that happening to one of our young'ns who might be water-skiing in the ditches or down the *Wacasassi*.

Grandpa Dewitt Watson

The picture above is of the late Grandpa Dewitt Watson. Grandpa Dewitt was so good at killing gators he didn't even need a light. He could sit on the bank and call a gator from wherever it was hiding. Dewitt could kill it, skin it, and be on his way before you knew it.

The Night Dewitt Escaped

The Game Commission wanted to catch Dewitt so bad, one night they set a trap for him. They stretched a cable across the river at the old tram crossing on Wacasassa, in an attempt to stop his airboat.

It's a miracle that he wasn't killed. If he hadn't seen the cable glistening in the moonlight, it would have not just stopped the airboat, it would have literally cut his head off. But God was merciful. Dewitt saw the cable just in time, swerved to miss it, sank the airboat, and *slipped home* through the woods. Anyway, the rivers were much safer back then.

Later on, when we finally got a pair of store bought water skis, I could take a boatload of teenagers down the Wacasassa and let them water ski right off of the mud bar on the end of Stafford's Island without worrying about gators. We'd stand on the mud flat on the outside of Stafford's Island and ski down the wide part of the river toward the mouth.

The day Glen Holmes lost his bathing suit

On one of those occasions, we were having a good time until I pulled Glen Holmes *clean outta* (this is not misspelled) his bathing suit. The water was so dark we never found his trunks. The girls in the boat had to close their eyes as we lifted Glen back into the boat, *butt naked.* We wrapped a towel around him, and headed back upriver to the fish camp to get him some clothes.

This is Glen Holmes, the son of Buford Holmes mentioned in chapter 2. The Holmes family was the first family we met in Levy county and they have been like our own family ever since.

This picture was taken at Dick Parnell's funeral on Tuesday, April 28, 2015

Liz's Narrow Escape

Our granddaughter, Liz (Keith) Yearty, also lives near the Wekiva. One day, when the tide was low, Liz was wading around in the Wekiva that runs behind her house. Her little dog was with her when suddenly she heard something behind her. She looked back and about ten feet away was a large alligator, about eight feet long, coming towards her with its mouth open. She got out of the water just in time to keep from being "gator bait."

Pictures by Liz Yearty

Our Granddaughter Liz (Keith) Yearty

Chapter 8

Everybody Went to Chiefland on Saturday

Back in the *good ole days*, it seems that everybody went to Chiefland on Saturdays, except during hunting season. During the hunting season, we would all be down at our hunting camps by late Friday night.

The first stop for men was the barber shop. We got our haircuts on Saturday and caught up on all of the news.

Back then, going to the barber shop in Chiefland was like going to college. The barber was an expert on politics, religion, sports, and anything else important. You could also learn just about every bit of gossip in the county if you'd just sit there, pretending to be reading a magazine, and keep your ears open.

Beauchamp's Hardware

The second stop for men was Beauchamp's. We might not need anything but we had to stop in, visit, and look around. If Beauchamp's didn't have it, they could order it. If they couldn't order it, we probably didn't need it. The best part of it all was *we could pay for it on time*. We couldn't have survived without Beauchamp's.

The One Arm Doctor

If we *took bad sick*, (*Order Creek* dialect), we could go up to Chiefland and see Dr. Farnell, the one-arm doctor. He could do as much with one arm as most doctors could do with two.

That good doctor lost his arm *dynamit'n* mullet down on the Wekiva. That, by the way, was one of the most effective methods of catching a mess of fish back then. You would stand on the bank and wait for a school of mullet to approach. When you saw the school coming, you would light the stick of dynamite, throw it in the water, and "bam." There would be mullet, bream, bass, warmouth perch and all kinds of stuff floating to the top. But one time, the good doctor held the dynamite too long and it exploded. It blew off one hand and most of one arm.

Chapter 9

Fishing in Levy County

I grew up on Spring Bayou in Tarpon Springs and have been fishing on the Gulf and the West Coast of Florida for 75 of my eighty-two years.

However, until we moved to Otter Creek, I hadn't been much further north than Hudson and the shallow rocks around Weekiwachee and Bayport.

Our first taste of fishing in our new world began when Murrell Watson and his older brother, Dewitt, took me to the flats between Wacasassa, the bombing range, and Cedar Key.

They also introduced me to the trout bait used by all of the old commercial fishermen, called *shiner tails*.

For you Yankee readers, "shiners" are what you call "sailor's choice" or "pinfish." To Florida Crackers and old timers, they are shiners," because that is what Adam named them.

Murrell Watson - Franklin Watson's Dad

Russell & Mrs. Goodbred

Another old timer who helped me improve my fishing skills was Mr. Russell Goodbred, a commercial fisherman. Mrs. Goodbred's mother was a full blooded Creek Indian.

The picture above is of Captain Jimmy Keith, Tuelah Keith, with Mr. and Mrs. Goodbred down at the old William's Landing Fish Camp in Gulf Hammock. Annie Kate (Goodbred) Berryhill, was their daughter.

William's Fish Camp

When we moved to Otter Creek back in 1954, we had to drive several miles down a sand road, from Otter Creek, past the checking station, and then to Williams Landing.

If you ever managed to get there without getting stuck (which was rare), you could fill a number three washtub with big redfish.

The Goodbreds operated the fish camp. They had some old rental boats and some old cabins. Mrs. Goodbred had a little coffee shop and the fishing was out of this world.

Ralph Green was also a guide and he taught me how to troll for redfish with a River Runt artificial "plug."

This is our son, Bill Keith in front of the pastorium in Otter Creek. Back in those days it was legal to keep the redfish like those in the picture above. We called them "Cobb Reds" and they were our favorites.

Bill was three years old when we moved to Otter Creek. Later, he served as the pastor of the Otter Creek Church for 18 years before becoming the pastor of the Countryside Baptist Church and school in Gainesville.

Afraid of the Flats

When we first moved to Otter Creek, very few of the "old timers" around Otter Creek fished out on the flats. They were afraid to go too far out. Most of them stayed inside the "L & M Stake," although a few daring souls went as far as the bombing range. The old timers thought the bombing range was close to the Florida Middle Grounds. I think some of them thought you would sail off of the edge of the earth if you went past the L & M stake.

Sandy and Jimmy

The next picture is yours truly with Captain Jim Keith and his sister, Sandy Keith Robertson, who were both born while we were living in Otter Creek.

We were bass fishing up Double Barrel Creek in this picture. We always fished the low tide (for bass) because the fish are out of the woods and back in the creek. Our family has been fishing the same area for half a century.

Big 25 HP "Kickers"

When we first moved to Otter Creek, we called outboard motors "kickers," and a 25 HP Evinrude was the biggest outboard motor made in America. It was rare back then to find a rental boat that would hold such a big outboard motor.

When Beauchamp's Hardware in Chiefland got in the first 25 horsepower Evinrude, folks drove to Chiefland from all over the county to see it.

Sam Standridge bought that big 25 Evinrude and took it to Otter Creek. Men who were sitting in front of the Suwannee Store would stop their whittling, spit, shake their heads and mutter: *"Only Sam Standridge would want a monster motor like that."*

Cane poles and shiner tails

Long before jig-heads, plastic tails, and popper corks, commercial fishermen in the Big Bend area caught trout with cane poles and shiner tails.

By the way, a "shiner" is what Yankees and transplants call "Pin-fish" or "Sailors-Choice."

Like we mentioned earlier, Florida Crackers have always called them "shiners" because that's what Adam named them.

The Crazy Man from Cedar Key

The experience of a life time happened one day while I was out on the flats between the Wacasassa and Cedar Key.

I saw an old commercial fisherman from over in Cedar Key, using a cane pole to catch speckled trout, and I thought the old man had lost his mind. It wasn't the cane pole that puzzled me as much as what he was doing with it!

This weather-beaten *old salt* was dressed in overhauls, wearing a straw hat, and fishing with a cane pole.

As I watched this old man, he would take that cane pole and beat *the heck out of the* water. He was making an awful commotion. To say that this attracted my attention is an understatement.

I thought he would scare all the fish away. Yet, he was catching trout left and right and I was catching nothing. It was the strangest thing I'd ever seen.

I always considered myself a pretty good fisherman. Having been born in Tarpon Springs, and having fished the Gulf Coast of Florida all of my life, I thought you had to be quiet to catch fish. I had been led to believe, if you talked above a whisper, scraped the bait bucket across the floor of the boat, or made any noise at all, you would scare all of the fish away and they wouldn't bite for a week.

Yet, here this old man was thrashing his pole around in the water and catching trout while I wasn't catching anything. I learned later that his was the basic, tried and proven method the commercial fishermen used to catch trout in the Big Bend area.

When I adopted that method myself, I began to catch fish liked I had never caught fish before.

Evidently the splashing and thrashing around with the cane pole excited the fish in that general area and they would come to see what's going on. Whatever the reason, the fact is, this method really works. If you decide to try it, here are some simple suggestions.

Catch a Shiner

The first thing you have to do is to catch a shiner and cut the shiner tails just right. Rig a small hook with a split shot sinker. Bait the hook with a piece of white bacon, shrimp, squid, or cut bait of any kind. Drop it down and before you know it, you will have a shiner on the line. No Cracker I knew ever bought shrimp.

Cut the Shiner in Half

The second step is to cut the shiner "just right." Take a sharp knife and cut the shiner at an angle from the front of the dorsal fin to the anal cavity.

This will give you a half-fish cut at an angle as in the picture.

If you don't cut the bait correctly you will catch *trash-fish* instead of trout.

Cut the Half into Two Equal Parts

The third step is to cut the lower half of the shiner into two equal parts. This makes two very attractive baits. Then, use the remainder of the shiner for bait to catch more shiners. This is so easy and inexpensive. All you need is a small piece of bacon to catch your first shiner. After that, you are in business."

Proper Rigging

You will need a long, stout, cane pole. For line, we recommend 20-30 pound test monofilament line with a swivel about three feet from the end. This will keep the line from twisting when the bait twirls around as it moves through the water.

We recommend large, long-shank hooks that are easy to grasp and remove quickly from the fish's mouth.

Calling up the Trout

When you are ready to do some serious fishing, bait your hook with a shiner tail, splash the tip of the pole in the water several times as vigorously as you can, and then whip your bait out there and hold on. *Florida Crackers* call this technique *"calling up the trout."*

The more noise you make the better it is. This technique undoubtedly led later to the development of popper corks, equalizers, and Cajun Thunders.

When you catch one trout, there are probably more of them in the same area. Therefore, it is important to remove the hook from the fish's mouth as fast as you can and throw it out again.

Drift

We usually drift while trout fishing. When drifting, it's a good idea to place a couple of split-shot sinkers above your hook to keep the bait down when the wind and tide are moving in the same direction.

Landing the Fish

Landing the fish with a long cane pole is another story altogether. This technique takes lots of practice. Have your video ready.

The old commercial fishermen I knew never used landing nets. They perfected the art of bringing the fish into the boat without lifting it out of the water until the last minute. I've seen them hook the fish, catch it between their legs, and throw their bait back out again in one smooth motion.

You will probably lose more fish than you keep at first. On some, you will snatch the hook right out of their tender mouths. On others, you will over-react and swing the poor trout into the air, over the boat, and into the water on the other side. It will be hilarious!

Believe me, it will be an unforgettable experience. Think of all the money you'll save. Try it! You might like it!

Believe me, it will be an unforgettable experience. Think of all the money you'll save. Try it! You might like it!

Mark the Spot

If you don't have a GPS, you can make an inexpensive marker out of a plastic milk jug with a line and a weight. Anytime you catch more than one fish, drop the marker on that spot.

When you catch a few fish and then drift awhile without catching any more, you've probably drifted past the "hot spot." That's the time to start your engine and go back to your marker-and make the same drift over again.

Sharks

We need to warn you ahead of time that you will probably catch a lot of small sharks using this method, so be ready for some fast action. You would be surprised how fast you can wear down a small shark on a twenty foot cane pole.

Note: The shark in the following picture *was not caught* on a cane pole, but it was caught on the flats out of Cedar key.

Tarpon

If you happen to hook a Tarpon, and sooner or later, you probably will, simply let him have the pole and all. It will eventually throw the hook and you can get your pole back.

Chapter 10

Hunting in Levy County

The Meeks family starts them out young.

From the time Tuelah and I left home to enter the ministry, until we moved to Otter Creek, neither of us had enjoyed many days off. We both had been working and going to school with no time to "play." Actually, neither of us had ever deer hunted before we moved to Otter Creek.

Up until that time, I was a quail hunter. I had two bird dogs and hunted all over Levy County. Two of my favorite spots were between Rocky Hammock and the Six Mile Still, and the area between what is now the Levy County Sheriff's office and the Bronson Road Baptist Church.

Hunting Season a Top Priority

When we moved to Otter Creek, we discovered that when hunting season came, nearly everything shut down and everybody went to the woods to hunt. We felt like we had died and gone to Heaven. However, some of our friends like Hershel and Red John didn't get too excited about the first week of hunting season, because they and some others hunted year round. I think I heard somebody say their motto was, *"If it was brown...it's down."*

Dixie County

Levy County was wild, but *not quite as wild* as Dixie County. Up *across the* river, deer hunters would take a pack of long-legged Walkers and drive the *Breedin' area* in broad open daylight. I saw it happen myself one year between Horse Shoe and Steinhatchee, on the Fourth of July.

Another thing about Dixie County was, you could look at a pickup truck and usually tell if the owner was from Dixie County. There would be a dog box and the CB antennae was always slanted back and down at an angle.

In my opinion, it took a brave soul to be a game warden in Dixie County.

Levy County

In Levy County, it was a little different. Usually there was mutual respect between the outlaws, the game wardens, and their families. They knew each other on a first-name basis and some had even married close kin. A game warden might chase a fire-hunter all over the hammock on

Saturday night and then their *young'ns* would still sit next to each other in church on Sunday Morning and ride the school bus to Bronson on Monday.

I remember one time a game warden (Grady) caught a fire hunter one night and as they wrestled together, the fire-hunter got shot in the foot. When it was all over, their wives still spoke and their children rode the school bus to Bronson together.

Whenever we had a poor hunting season with just a few deer, the home folks usually blamed it on "*That bunch from Tampa,*" not on the fire hunters. That's the way it was in the good old days in Otter Creek.

Our First Hunting Season

Our first hunting season on Otter Creek was a real adventure. Buford Homes and Sam Standridge persuaded us to go with them down to Camp E, on the back side of Gulf Hammock. We had never been there before and looked forward to seeing the "camp."

When we arrived at "Camp E" there was nothing there but a pitcher pump on the old tram road. Our youngest daughter Sandy was only eight weeks old at that time.

Tuelah, our three children, Dottie, Mrs. Liza and the women folks slept in the back of a large truck covered with a piece of canvas.

Bufford, Donald Homes and I slept in the bed of Mr. Buford's hide truck. It was like placing three books in a crowded bookshelf. To say we were cold is an understatement.

Sam and Dottie Standridge

Later on, we began to hunt regularly with Buford Holmes and Sam Standridge. When Sam and Buford decided to build a hunting camp at Camp D, Sam built a little cabin for the preacher and his family and never charged us a dime for it. We have hours of precious memories in that old camp site when our kids were young.

Elwin, Betty Jo, Dottie, and Sam Standridge

On another occasion our 1950 Oldsmobile literally gave up the ghost." Sam told me to take it down to Willie Berryhill's garage. Willie completely overhauled it and Sam paid for it himself.

We will never be able to repay Sam and Dottie for their kindness to us while we lived in Otter Creek.

Later on, Sam Standridge also bought the first 25 HP outboard motor in Levy County. He was very generous and we borrowed that motor on many occasions.

There was only one problem. The rental boats at the fish camp were not made for such large motors and we had to be extra careful with such a large motor.

Willie and Annie Kate Berryhill holding Baby Regina

When we moved from Otter Creek to Gainesville in 1959, it was literally like moving from heaven to hell. The people in Levy County had been so nice to us it was a rude shock to be treated differently in Gainesville. There were a few exceptions, but the people in Gainesville were so mean to our family, the only way I survived was to go back to our hunting camp in Gulf Hammock as often as possible.

Willie and Annie Kate Berryhill owned some property near the old Williams' Landing, and they allowed us to build a campsite there without charge. We hunted there for years. The next picture was taken as the boys and I started building our own camp. It was our refuge.

The Old Keith Camp

We will forever be indebted to Willie and Annie Kate for allowing us to build a campsite on their land. Our children spent many memorable nights on that site.

The next picture is a sketch of our old campsite down near the fish camp on Wacasassa, drawn by Dave Mulligan.

Beverly Hillbillies

Later on, after moving to Gainesville, we were too poor to have a truck, and a 4x4 was out of the question. So we took an old 1946 Chevrolet, cut most of the body off, built a dog box, put on some large tires, and made a hunting buggy. We could carry the dogs and the kids in the large dog box.

One day when I was leaving Gainesville for the camp, one of our church members (G.K. Anderson) saw me and told somebody, "I saw the preacher leaving for Gulf Hammock and he reminded me of the Beverly Hillbillies."

The Preacher Keith Road

When we moved down to Cape Canaveral, Florida in 1968-1969, we still hunted out of our old camp near Willie and Annie Kate's place.

On the first week of hunting season, 1968, my best beagle died on Sunday. I only had two dogs and Ruth Revels had boarded them all year long. That meant that we were facing the first week of hunting season with no dogs.

John Yearty came to the Rescue.

John had a few beagles that ran deer every day. So, he loaned me one of his little dogs. Tuelah and I went down towards what we call the "smokehouse" in what is now the Fiber Factory hunting club. I turned John's little beagle loose and she began trailing. It wasn't long before she "jumped."

The only bad thing the deer was heading north and I knew it would cross Wekiva and be gone. Suddenly I got excited. The deer didn't cross the creek but turned back and I knew it would cross the tram somewhere between me and the river. I eased along listening, and then suddenly, the little buck hit the tram and made the mistake of his life. He stopped and looked at me. I raised my little .44 magnum carbine and knew the Lord had provided the Keith family with some good old Levy County "fast food."

That's how the Preacher Keith Road got its name.

Tweeter Road

Another interesting thing happened that day. The Supervisor of the land we were hunting on named that road the *Preacher Keith Road*. He wanted to also name one road after my wife, Tuelah. He, like a lot of people, couldn't spell "Tuelah," so he named it *Tweeter Road*.

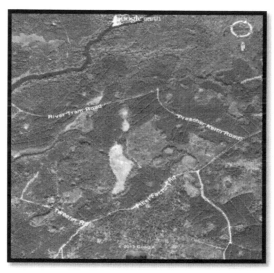

Those two roads still bear our names today on Google Earth.

This picture is Tuelah (my wife and editor) and our son, Jimmy, in front of the old checking station on the Buck Island grade. This was her first turkey.

Fifty years later, our family is still enjoying the woods and waters of Levy County.

Sam Owens Waiting on the Dogs

Jim Keith with a nice Hog

Here I am with a nice Hog

Author's wife, Tuelah, waiting on the dogs

Our Granddaughter, Michelle (Keith) Meeks, warming up her children's lunch in her Redneck Microwave.

Chapter 11

Whatever happened to Old Cush?

Old Cush got off of the bus half-way between Otter Creek and Cedar Key, walked south into the Hammock, and nobody has ever heard from him again. But wait! We're getting ahead of our story.

Old Cush was one of the colorful characters I met when I came to Otter Creek to become the young pastor of the Otter Creek First Baptist Church. Old Cush was a real character. He had no family and we never knew where he actually lived.

Everybody called him "Cush." Nobody knows if "Cush" was his first name or his last name. Nobody seems to remember where he came from or how old he was.

All we know is that one day Old Cush just up and disappeared, *but again, I'm getting ahead of the story.*

Some folks in the barber shop in Chiefland said Old Cush lived under the Otter Creek Bridge on US 19. Others said he slept behind Mrs. Julia's store in Otter Creek. Nobody really knows. We've learned since then that Cush actually owned a little shack down in Cedar Key.

Deer Tongue

Cush sold deer tongue for a living. Deer tongue is a ground plant that grows wild in the piney-woods. It is shaped like the tongue of a deer. It has a sweet aroma used in vanilla extract and some smoking tobacco.

Grunt Worms

Cush also grunted worms. There are two kinds of fishing worms: ***grunt worms and wigglers***. Wigglers are found in damp ground in the ditches and around the back side of any wash-house where you emptied the wash tubs. Grunt worms are also called earthworms. They are longer than wigglers and they live in the piney woods.

To grunt worms you drive a wooden stake into the ground about a foot. Then you take a flat piece of iron like a leaf from a car spring. Rub the flat iron across the wood stake and it makes a fierce vibration that drives the worms crazy. You can grunt for a minute or two and worms will come a-crawling to the surface to escape the torment below. It takes a team to grunt worms for a living.

One person can grunt and the others pick up. The high dollar grunters are usually a family with *a lot of young'ns*. The daddy would usually grunt while momma and the young'uns picked up.

Cush's Cart

Old Cush had made a little *push cart* with bicycle wheels and a broom handle for a tongue, to help him gather deer tongue. You could see Cush just about anywhere in the woods *a-pulling* his old cart and gathering deer-tongue.

Played the Fiddle

Some nights Old Cush would appear out of nowhere and show up at Lawrence Lee's gas station at the crossroads and play his fiddle. He would get an RC Cola crate, set it up on end by the free air hose, sit on the crate, take his fiddle out of his croaker sack he always carried, begin tapping his foot *and a-playing* some old folk-song or mountain-like ballad.

One of his favorite tunes was about *"an old Blue-gum N***er with a nose like a brogan shoe. . . ."* He seemed to like that tune because he *played it a powerful lot*.

The 1950 Hurricane

A terrible hurricane swept through Levy County in 1950 devastating the low-lying coastal area. Old Cush was in Cedar Key at that time and it was too late to catch the bus out. Otter Creek was a long walk.

Old Cush survived the storm by going out to the high ground near the Cedar Key cemetery, digging himself a hole like a gopher, and crawling in it. As the howling winds swept in from the Gulf and the waters flooded the coastal marsh-land, old Cush was all hunkered down in his gopher-hole.

When the storm was over, Cush climbed out of his hole, dried out his clothes in the bright sun, and went on about his business. Cush never did find his little deer-tongue cart. Somebody down at the Suwannee store said they heard that somebody had found Cush's cart up in a sweet-gum tree near the California Swamp near Shired Island. Nobody knew for sure.

Cush Just Disappeared

Back in the good old days an old Greyhound bus ran from Gainesville to Cedar Key on SR 24 every day. It would come through Otter Creek every evening and stop at the intersection by Lee's Standard station, then proceed on down to Cedar Key where the driver would spend the night and return to Gainesville the next morning. Old Cush would often catch the bus to Cedar key. Then one day Old Cush *just up-n-disappeared*. Nobody has ever seen or heard from him since.

Folks began to try to *figger-out* what had happened to him.

Greyhound Bus Driver

The last person to see him was the driver of the Greyhound bus. The Driver said that when Cush climbed aboard the bus in Otter Creek, he had his 12 gauge shotgun with him. As was customary when taking a gun on the bus, Cush broke his double-barrel shotgun in two, stuck it in his croaker sack and got on board.

Dunton Spur

Down near the old Mack Hodges place, also called *Dunton Spur* by the old timers, Old Cush asked the driver to stop the bus. Cush got out, walked into the woods in the direction of Jackson Oak, and has never been seen again.

Several people said they had heard him say that when it was his time to go, he would go out in the woods, find a gator hole, and climb in, and let the gators dispose of his old body. Perhaps that's what happened to Ole Cush.

Perhaps someday, some hunter will be easing through the hammock and stumble across an old rusted out double barrel shotgun and a few bones. It's probably Old Cush.

Or maybe somebody will kill a big old gator and cut him open looking for dog-collars in his belly.

If they find an old brogan shoe or a piece of a fiddle, it probably belonged to old Cush.

Picture provided by Liz Yearty

Chapter 12

Murder on Main Street

Crazy Jake wasn't really crazy, but he was definitely scary. Everybody kept out of his way and nobody dared "cross" him.

Why did people refer to him as "Crazy Jake?" We know this will be hard for you to believe, but this man, Jake Yearty, had killed a Black man, on Main Street in Otter Creek, simply for owing him 35 cents.

He would have certainly gone to the electric chair for this crime but his father, Will, persuaded the court to declare him insane instead.

Jake Hated His Father

You would think that Jake would have thanked his father for saving his life, but he didn't. He hated his father for this act and they were enemies for the rest of Jake's life. The hatred was so intense that his father, *Ole Pal* Yearty, had to move out of his house and live with another son, John, down in Gulf Hammock, while Jake spent the rest of his life living with his mother in Otter Creek. We always got along with Jake even though we didn't have any dealing with him. We, like everybody else simply stayed out of his way.

Happy Ending

The story does, however, have a happy ending. As the years passed, it seemed that no one had seen Jake for awhile.

His brother, John Yearty, from Gulf Hammock decided to drive up to Otter Creek and check on him. When they arrived in Otter Creek, they found Jake sprawled out on the floor. They had no idea of how long he had been there, but they immediately took him to the Veteran's hospital for emergency treatment.

During his recovery, Jake was reconciled to his brother John. In the process he told John that he had an outboard motor and a Jon boat in his garage in Otter Creek and he wanted John's son, Danny to have it.

Motor Still in the Carton

When they arrived at Jake's house in Otter Creek, they immediately went to his garage to look for the outboard motor. They didn't see one until they noticed a large cardboard box standing in the corner. They opened the large box and inside they found a brand new, 2 HP air-cooled outboard motor that had never been used. It was odd looking and had a weird, gold colored cowling.

They took the boat and new motor down to Wekiva and Danny took it on its maiden voyage. Danny told me that just before he reached the fish camp, he began to think about that weird golden cowling. Danny was afraid some of his friends would laugh at him, so he stopped the motor, took off the cowling, and threw it into the dark waters of the Wacasassa, never to be seen again.

Jake Yearty wrote this book

Chapter 13

Moonshine Mary

Moonshine whiskey was popular back in the past, but the folks in Levy County were not quite as bad as the folks were up in Baker County.

My friend, Jerry Milton, told me that up in McClenney, where he was raised, nearly everybody was involved in making moon-shine. Jerry said that in Baker County, moon-shiners would sometimes keep their *young'ns* out of school during the busy season to wax cans and help keep the family business going. The fastest cars in the county always belonged to the moonshiners.

Moonshine Stills

Down in Levy County, moonshine stills were scattered through-out the woods, especially in Devil's Hammock where the river runs for miles through a thick hammock.

We taught our kids to get away as fast as they could if they happened to come upon a moon-shine still in the woods. We'd heard tales about people *gettin' shot* for just snooping around a still.

Moonshine Mary

Moonshine Mary was a friend of ours. She was an old Black woman who lived down in Ellzey. She rode in a wagon, pulled by a thirty-one year old horse named Johnny. Mary would often pass our house on the way to the Suwannee store in Otter Creek.

Mary was Black and we were White.

Mary made moonshine, had served time in prison, and I was a Baptist preacher.

However, I knew my kids were safe *a-ridin*, with Moonshine Mary and Old Johnny.

That's the way things were in the *good ole days*.

Chapter 14

Pistol Packing Grandma

Who would ever believe that grandmother would shoot sour oranges off of *a grand young'uns* heads with a pistol? Well, Grandma McCreary could, and she did so on a regular basis, on an island in Cedar Key. But wait. I'm getting ahead of my story. Let's start at the beginning.

Giovanni Dominic Delaino

Giovanni Dominic Delaino served in the Austrian Navy for twelve years and had come to America during the War Between the States. No one knows for sure if Dominic served in that war, but we do know he had been stationed in Key West before moving to Cedar Key.

It is believed that he jumped ship from the Austrian Navy while it was docked at Key West. He got a small sail boat and sailed up the coast to Sop Choppy where he met Martha Carter, a native of Wakulla County and brought her back to Scale Key

Scale Key

Together they raised six children on the island. Dominic did just about anything he could to scratch out a living for his family.

According to his daughter-in-law, Mary Ann Delaino, he fished, gathered oysters, caulked boats, pruned grape arbors, raised chickens, and had a garden.

The West coast of Florida abounded with food in those days. All one had to do was cut it, catch it, pick it up, or kill it.

In fact, I have come to believe that the Garden of Eden must have been located somewhere in Levy County, probably somewhere between Shell Mound and Mo Quick's old place, on Wekiva Run.

McCreary's Cove

If you look at the modern nautical charts of the Cedar Key area, you will notice there's a cove on North Key named "McCrary" Cove.

They misspelled *"McCreary"* on the charts, but at least the cove still bears the name of the family which once lived on that tiny island.

Picture Courtesy of Google Earth

Some time back in the 1800's, Uncle Robbie McCreary, as he was called, settled there and raised his family. Soon after coming to the island, Uncle Robbie married Katherine Delaino, one of the six children of Giovanni Dominic Delano.

1896 Tidal Wave

In 1896, Dominic's 13 year old son, William Peter (Evelyn Yearty's Grandfather), was fishing with his brother-in-law, Robbie McCreary, when the storm hit. Miraculously they both survived although the storm devastated the west coast of Florida.

Life on the Island

Anyway, back to our story about Grandma Katherine. Each Fourth of July, friends and relatives from the Coastal area would sail or pole out to celebrate the holidays on McCreary Island. They would feast on venison, clams, mullet, swamp cabbage, and wild hog.

Shooting Skills

Grandma McCreary was a legend in the Big Bend area. She carried a pistol everywhere she went.

On holidays like the Fourth of July, after a sumptuous meal, they tell us that Grandma Katherine would amaze the folks with her skills with the pistol.

They tell us that she would line up her *young'ns* in the order of their birth.

Then, she would place an orange on each one's head, and then would back off a piece and commence to shoot the oranges right off of each one's head *without cut'n a hair.*

Wild Bill Hickok

We learned recently, that Wild Bill Hickok was so impressed with Grandma's shooting skills he actually came to Levy County and tried to persuade her to join him and travel with him in his Wild West Show. She was "that good." She declined the offer.

Our Kinfolks

The Keith family is now related to both the McCreary and the Yearty families.

Our grandson, Billy Keith married Ginny Yearty, who is the great-great niece of Grandma Katherine, the pistol-packing grandma. Katherine was Ginny's great-great aunt, who was Will Delainos' sister.

Ginny's mother, Evelyn (Walwrath) Yearty, was the granddaughter of William Peter Delaino, who was Katherine's brother.

Our son, David, married Sherri McCreary, the daughter of Jody McCreary, the great grandson of Rob McCreary.

The next picture shows some of Grandma Katherine's descendants playing on the same island where she used to display her skills with that .22 pistol.

Our son, David, married Sherri McCreary, is the daughter of Jody McCreary, who is pictured on the next page posing with that very same pistol Grandma used to shoot the sour oranges off of her grandchildren's heads.

North Key Today

The island is now called North Key. This particular beach is my favorite picnic spot. It's called McCreary's Cove on the nautical maps.

They tell us that Grandpa and some of the clan are actually buried somewhere on the island, but the one-legged man in Cedar Key who knew where the graves were, died and nobody remembered to mark the sites.

Some of Pistol Packing Grandma's descendants are still alive and can vouch for the authenticity of this story.

Katherine's Descendants

The Delaino's, Wadley's, and Yearty's still live in Cedar Key and in Gulf Hammock.

Jody McCreary, the great-grandson of Rob McCreary, lives in Tarpon Springs and recently bought some property on Wekiva right below the Yearty's.

The following picture is Jody holding the very pistol Grandma Katherine used.

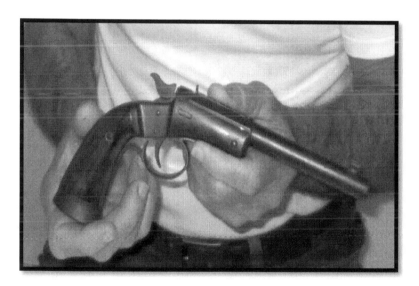

Chapter 15

A Country Baptism

We've never really lost anybody at a baptism, nor has anybody drowned or been bitten by a snake. But in the case of Mrs. Mulligan, we came close. It all happened one Sunday afternoon while we were baptizing in the Wekiva

Run behind the old community church building in Gulf Hammock.

The weather was hot, the water was cold, and the current was fairly swift. I took Mrs. Mulligan by the hand and led her down into the water.

The bottom was fairly rough and I had to help steady her as she made it to the middle of the creek. All went well until I had baptized her and she began to try to make it back to the creek bank.

Just about the time I let go of her hand, she slipped and began rolling over and over as the current began moving her toward the bend in the creek. John Yearty jumped in the creek, shoes and all, and rescued Mrs. Mulligan before she rounded the bend.

Kill the Snake

We still baptize in Wekiva as often as we can. Our son, Bill Keith, who is now the pastor of the Countryside Baptist Church of Gainesville, also lives on the beautiful Wekiva Run.

One beautiful Sunday afternoon we all gathered at the creek bank for the occasion. As we looked in the water, some of the women were a little nervous because a large water snake was curled up in the stumps at the water's edge.

Now we all know water-snakes are harmless, but there was a Yankee woman there who had never been to a country baptism before, and she was in for a big surprise.

Sam Owens

All of us local folks know those snakes are harmless but some of the women folks were a bit nervous.

So, we paused for a few minutes while Sam Owens got his 12 gauge shotgun out of his truck, shot the snake, and cleaned out the baptistry.

The boy in the next picture, waded out, grabbed the dead snake, put him on the bank and the baptism continued. This was nothing out of the ordinary for us Levy County folks but that *Yankee woman* could not believe her eyes.

Chapter 16

The Fastest Deputy in Levy County

Deputy Ray Burnette was a legend around Gulf Hammock. He lived in Gulf Hammock and drove a 1956 Ford with four barrel carbs, *Smitty mufflers*, standard shift, and overdrive. To say it was fast is an understatement. It was "hot!"

50 mph in First Gear

This may be hard for you younger folks to believe, but those straight shift cars with overdrive could actually run 50 mph in first gear. You could put the car in first gear, step on the gas and run it up to around 30 mph. Then, let off of the accelerator and let the overdrive drop in and hit it again. Most of those cars in those days would hide the 120 mph speedometer.

There is no way to estimate the money Ray brought into the Levy County coffers by catching speeders on US 19. It was like hunting in a zoo.

Flat Branch

Back then there was nothing between Chiefland and Crystal River and Ray would hide on the East side of US 19 by Flat Branch, waiting for his prey. Drivers would leave Chiefland and head south. By the time they got to Flat Branch, they were *really cruising*.

Then came Charlie

One night, my friend, the late Charlie Richelieu and his family, had been visiting us in Otter Creek. Charlie had a 1956 Chevrolet stick shift, overdrive and power pack. His car and Ray's would both hide their speedometers.

Well, you can guess the rest of the story. Ray was at his usual hiding place at Flat Branch and Charlie had just left Otter Creek.

By the time Charlie reached Flat Branch, heading back to St. Petersburg, he was literally flying.

Ray took off after Charlie, and finally caught him. But he had to chase him all the way to Crystal River to do it. When he pulled him over in Crystal River, the radiator on Ray's Ford was steaming.

Naturally, Charlie didn't have enough money for the fine, nor did he want to go to jail in Bronson. So Charlie pleaded with Ray and finally persuaded Ray to take his .22 magnum pump rifle as security until he could scrape up the money and get it back up to Bronson. I'm not sure Charlie ever made it back to Bronson or not.

Chapter 17

Junior Williams and the Lucky Ticket

Junior and Philene Williams lived across the street from Buford and Liza Holmes. Junior and his dad had a filling station located where the Otter Creek Post Office now stands.

Historical Event

Junior actually made history one day by winning a brand new boat, motor, and trailer. If my memory serves me correctly, Junior and Philene had attended some kind of outing up at Kingsley Lake in Camp Blanding.

Like others, Junior had purchased a $1.00 ticket on a complete boat and trailer package, and like the rest of us, never dreamed of having the winning ticket. But, lo and behold, when the winning number was announced, it was his.

How did Junior's win change the history of Otter Creek? Up until that time, the only two people in Otter Creek who owned boats were Grady Phelps, the Game Warden, and

John Moody who owned a filling station where Hershel's store now stands.

There were only two outboard motors in town at that time. The Game Warden had a 15 HP Evinrude and a boat. Sam Standridge had a monster 25 HP Evinrude and that was it. The only other boat in Otter Creek belonged to John Moody, and it was a flat bottom, homemade aluminum boat.

I didn't personally know anyone in Levy County who owned a pair *of store bought water skies*. I had learned to ski on a pair of skis my brother Louis made of plywood with the bottom cut out of rubber wading boots, stapled on to the skis for our feet.

My brother later bought a pair of real skis from Sears and Roebuck and those are the very skis I taught most of the kids in Otter Creek to ski on by pulling them down SR 24 behind my 1950 Pontiac.

When Junior won that 16 foot plywood boat with a Mark 55 Mercury motor, everybody began to get the boat fever.

Buford Holmes

Buford Holmes was next. He got the fever and bought a brand new 16 foot plywood runabout with a brand new 35HP motor.

Lewis Renfroe

"Mr. Louis" was not to be outdone. He ordered a fiberglass "Crosby" hull with round chimes. It would turn on a dime, running wide open, without cavitating. He then went to Baird Hardware in Gainesville and bought the largest outboard made in America at that time. It was a six cylinder in line 60 HP Mercury. It was truly revolutionary. We can say the outboard revolution had come to Otter Creek.

Beauchamp's to the Rescue

The Keith family had to get in on the revolution. I went up to Beauchamp's in Chiefland and they sold me a used 25 HP Evinrude with an electric start, and sold it to me "on time."

Sam Standridge

Sam Standridge was not to be outdone either. He bought a 16 foot Stamas plywood hull and put twin 35 HP Evinrudes on it. That was just the beginning.

Fun in the Sun

From that time forward, every Saturday when the weather permitted, we and our friends would gather somewhere on the Suwannee River to fellowship, water ski and then grill hamburgers.

There was a public launching ramp at the Fanning Springs Bridge and a nice public ramp at Fowlers' Bluff. Those were some precious times.

Chapter 18

Norwood Ishee Day

Many of you have never heard of Norwood Ishee. At one time his was one of the most popular names in Levy County. Norwood worked at the courthouse in Levy County. Norwood was not a judge. Neither was he an attorney. Nor did he serve as a County Commissioner. Norwood was the custodian of the Levy County courthouse.

How did Norwood become so famous? You have to live in Levy County to really understand this. One day the employees of the courthouse agreed that they needed some time off from their grueling schedule. They decided that they would declare Thursdays an official county holiday. They agreed to celebrate Thursday by having a fish fry at the courthouse. They named the holiday "Norwood Ishee Day." The idea immediately became popular and before long, stores and businesses all over Levy County began closing and people looked forward each Thursday to just haul off and have some fun.

Chapter 19

John and Imogene Yearty

The Yeartys were always kind to us. They were members of the church in Otter Creek, and John's father, Will Yearty, (called "Ole Pal") served as the Treasurer of the church.

Back in those days the mill was still operating and the commissary was on the East side of US 19. The old train that was used to pull the lumber from the hammock can still be seen at the wayside park in Gulf Hammock.

John owned a large tract of land, bordering Wekiva, in Gulf Hammock, and he also managed the Pat-Mac filling station in Gulf Hammock, where the old Circle K was for a while.

John and Imogene were good to us. We were always welcome to swim at their "landing" and John allowed us to hunt on some property North of Wekiva that borders the road that now runs from Gulf Hammock to the fish camp and boat ramp. There was no road there back then and we had to reach this hunting area by boat.

The Yearty's were kind to us in more practical ways. We would always spend the first week of hunting season in our old camp on Willie Berryhill's property. As you know, hunting season always comes in the winter months. Since we had no bathroom or shower at the hunting camp, we would heat water over the open fire and bathe in a washtub. On days that were not so cold, we would actually bathe at the launching ramp at Williams Landing.

I remember one cold November, we had been at our camp for about a week and it had been too cold to bathe at the boat ramp. We were in great need of a real bath. It just so happened that we had stopped by the Yearty's house for something and they invited us to come in and take a real bath in their tub with hot running water. That hot bath was one of the greatest blessings in my life.

Chapter 20

Dick Parnell, George Bird, & Old Rattler

Update: When we were doing the final edit on this book, this man, Dick Parnell, one of my dearest friends, went to be with the Lord (4/25/15). RIP my dear brother.

I have great memories of George and Polly bird. The Birds were not pioneer Levy County families. They had moved up from Hillsborough County near Tampa.

George and Polly had owned the *Bird Fish Camp* on the Hillsborough River. They sold it, bought more property, improved it, and finally sold out and moved up to Levy County, where they purchased approximately 600 acres of land east of highway 19 in Gulf Hammock.

There was George, Polly, Stevie Byrd, and Danny Snider, George's nephew.

What was so enjoying about George and Polly is that they had horses we could hunt off of. Now, you can hunt off of any horse, but shooting off a horse is another matter. George had horses you could *shoot off of*, and we did.

When I was a kid, growing up in Tarpon Springs, I wanted a horse so bad I would have gladly traded my little brother and sisters for a horse. I am glad now that opportunity never came.

George also had some pretty good dogs. And although I didn't own a horse, George generously invited me to hunt with him and the boys on a number of occasions.

Steve Bird told me (November 5, 2013) that I really impressed him by my shooting. He said he remembers me throwing a can or bottle up in the air and hitting it with my 30.30 lever action Winchester.

German Island

One of my favorite drives was in a tract we refer to as Stavola, on the East side of US 19 just above Gulf Hammock. It borders the south edge of the McGee Branch Hunt Club.

George and I would take the horses across Wekiva and drive north toward what is now McGee. There was a section of high ground in there we called German Island. It was named "German Island" because some Germans had actually lived there years ago.

It is close to where (former Sheriff) Johnny Smith's tall stand is (or was), and we would *always jump* deer in there. Those deer just loved to lay up there and usually a nice buck or two would be in the bunch. We would have our standers waiting at places we knew the bucks would cross.

Power Line

One of my fondest memories was the day we had trailed a nice buck from US 19 (behind Frankie Couch's place), east, all the way to the power line, where the wise old buck gave our dogs the slip.

Dick Parnell

We were about to give up when we ran into Dick Parnell who had a little Beagle named "Rattler" that belonged to his Uncle Louis Baldree. That little Beagle, with a broken tail, had the coldest nose in Levy County.

We put old Rattler on the place where our dogs had lost it and sure enough, it wasn't long before his little tail went to wagging and he began to open. It wasn't long before our dogs began to get excited over the fresh scent. We crossed the power line and headed further east.

All of sudden, we reached a fence and George and I had to leave our horses. The trail was getting hotter by the minute and George and I were nearly out of breath, but we knew that old buck would get up at any moment.

I noticed that each time we reached a cypress pond, the old buck would go straight through and try to lose the dogs in the water.

The Buck Circled Pond

This happened several times and then I noticed something. We approached another cypress swamp and this time, instead of going straight in the trees, the old buck had circled around to the right. Our dogs were worn out and so were we. That old buck was smart but this time, but he hadn't fooled me.

I Knew His Trick

I told George I was going to stay right there on the West end of the cypress pond while he and the dogs followed the sign. I was right! The dogs followed the trail where the old buck had circled and then I heard them enter the pond from the other end. All of sudden, the dogs went crazy! The buck had jumped and the race was on. It was coming straight for me.

Sure enough, there he came, out of the thicket and straight for me. I cocked back the hammer on my Winchester 30.30, put my open sights on his chest, about 30 yards away, and said to myself, "You're Mine!" "Click!" NOTHING!

What's going on? I had forgotten to put a live round in the chamber. I had a magazine full, but for safety reasons, I never put a live round in the chamber while riding the horse, until I was ready to shoot.

Emptied my 30.30

I jacked one in the chamber and emptied my trusty old 30.30 as Mr. Buck high tailed it out of the danger zone.

Dick Parnell was still back on the power line and he had heard all of the shooting and began to smile. He just knew we would be along shortly dragging the deer out to the power line.

While he was sitting there smiling, he happened to look North on the power line just in time to see Mr. Buck, without a scratch, walking slowly back across it.

That wouldn't be the last time I lost a shirttail.

Chapter 21

Mrs. Thelma and the Phelps' Store

Long before anyone thought of 7-11 or Jiffy stores, Mrs. Thelma Phelps ran a little country store in Otter Creek where the road turns left off of SR 24 and takes you to main street in Otter Creek.

Thelma was a widow and had a house full of children. Grady and Dale were grown when we arrived in Otter Creek, and Dale, Darwin (Dirt), Sue, Gary, and Little Joe, were still living at home.

Three of the Phelps boys: Grady, Dale, and Gary, later served as Game Wardens. Grady retired as a Colonel, and was the second in command in the State of Florida. Gary, the youngest of the three, retired as Major. Dale left the game commission and worked in publishing until retirement.

Train Wreck

While Thelma's husband, Grady Sr. was still alive, he caused a lot of excitement in Otter Creek one day. There had been a train wreck over in Archer, and Grady Sr. ran down to the Otter Creek School.

He arrived when the children were out at recess. Grady Sr. cranked up the yellow school bus, blew the horn, loaded the children up from the playground and drove them to Archer to see the train wreck.

When the teachers rang the bell for the kids to come in from recess, all of the kids were gone and so was the bus.

To say that Grady caused some excitement in Levy County is an understatement.

His reason for this strange episode was: ***"Children don't often have the opportunity to see a real train wreck."***

They Almost Drowned Little Gary (By Bill Keith)

Some of the more famous people to come out of Otter Creek were the Phelps brothers. Later when the movies about Wyatt Earp were popular it always brought the Phelps brothers to my mind. They were wild and fearless young men that grew up roaming the woods and waters there in Otter Creek. Their father had passed away about a year before we arrived in 1954.

My father was about the same age as the three older brothers and immediately developed great friendships with them, and started hunting, fishing, and other outdoor activities. They enjoyed the fact that their new young preacher (my dad) was as bold and brave as they were!

Before his death, Mr. Phelps and his family had been a part of the Otter Creek Baptist Church for many years before my father arrived. He had taught his family to be God-fearing and honest.

The Phelps had four boys and one girl. Her name was Sue Phelps. And she was one of the prettiest little black haired girls I'd ever seen! I was 6 or 7 but sure did notice that teenager! Her older brothers were: Grady, Dale, Darwin (nicknamed "Dirt"), Gary, Sue, and Little Joe.

Their sweet mother, Mrs. Thelma, ran a general store at the corner of Highway 24 and 3rd Street. She also cut hair and did a little doctoring for the sick as well. Like all the stores in our tiny little town, Mrs. Thelma probably gave more away through unpaid charge tabs than she ever made in the way of real income! The truth was that most of the residents there were at or below poverty level! But that didn't seem to bother any of us!

When Mrs. Minnie, the county shot lady would come to give vaccinations to all the children in the community, it was done at Phelps's store. Cars would line up down highway 24 waiting their turn. You could tell it was shot day because of all the cars and all the crying *young'uns!*

No one but my sister, Sissy, liked the shots! Why she liked them we'll never know! Back then the needles were not disposable, but were sharpened by hand and used over-and-over!

One day when the Phelps boys were real young they went swimming down at Otter Creek, about ½ mile north of their store. Upon arriving back home after a couple hours of swimming, one of the boys said, *"Momma, Gary can hold his breath longer than any of us!"* She asked, "How can that be, he's only 5?" He replied. *"We just hold him down longer!"* When Mrs. Thelma heard that she about killed her older boys.

It wasn't long after my dad arrived in Otter Creek that the water skiing craze took off in Florida. The closest river was the Wacasassa River, six miles south of Otter Creek in Gulf Hammock. If you rode down it in a boat tomorrow it looks almost the same as it did 60 years ago, except now there are alligators all up and down the river. They weren't as plentiful back then, a story I will tell you about on another day

One day Dad and the Phelps boys decided to go skiing in the Wacasassa. They didn't have any skis so they borrowed the door off Mrs. Phelps wash house and drilled a hole in one end for the rope. They then would tie the rope to the boat and pull each other up and down the river. The driver had to sit in the back to steer the motor. Most all the motors back then had "tiller steering".

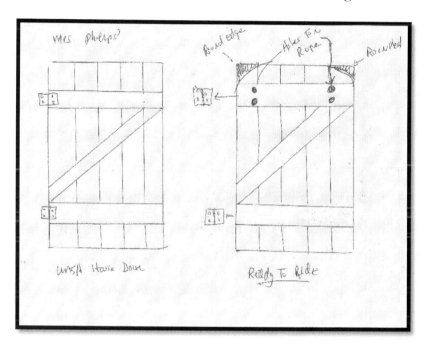

The river is pretty narrow in places and some of the limbs of the trees hang low out over the water. The driver would watch the river in front of the boat, while the rider would sit on the front of the boat and watch the skier, in case they fell off. Bad things would happen when both driver and rider were looking back and not watching where they were going!

One day my dad was driving with Gary Phelps sitting up on the bow, both looking backwards, when dad ran him right up under a low hanging branch which hit him right in the back! It hurt him pretty bad, so dad and his brothers helped him get off at a little deserted spot on the shore line, miles from nowhere, called Burn's Landing. He lay there writhing in pain until they got finished with their turns skiing. They then loaded Gary up and hauled him back home, alive, but badly bruised and scratched up! He lived.

When the ditches would flood, they would almost come over the road at times. This looked like a perfect place to practice their water skiing. By then they had acquired or borrowed some real skis and would pull each other behind the car down the ditches.

Gary told me he pulled dad in that old Pontiac up to about 65 miles per hour one time before he fell off and skipped across the water for about 50 yards. He lived too!

Like I said, these boys were wild and reckless! But they were good young men! And my dad was one of them! But their search for adventure and fun didn't deter them from loving the Lord and loving their families!

Everything they did or tried was something that had family involved in some fashion or another.

We were all fairly poor compared to worldly standards, but we were rich when it came to family and community.

Chapter 22

The Old Watson Place

Franklin Watson and his father, Murrell Watson

By Franklin Watson

I can still see it clearly in my mind from stories my dad told about his Grandfather to me as a boy. William T. Watson stood on his back porch when through the light layer of fog that floated a couple of feet off the ground; he noticed some movement in the back corner of the field. It was close to the area where deer came to feed in the early morning, and it looked like a couple of small deer moving around.

Traded with Indians

After watching for a couple of minutes, he recognized that it was two dogs belonging to his neighbors, Creek Indians who lived near him in the area known as Gulf Hammock. He knew that soon one or more of them would be climbing over the fence, making their way up to the house. It was only a few minutes when they appeared out of the timber line.

Traded with Loggers

William made a business out of trading with the hammock neighbors and particularly the loggers at the Patterson & MacInnis Timber Company logging camps in Gulf Hammock (Pat - Mac, as they were known in those days).

The Indians regularly traded with him for meat, dry goods, fruit and vegetables as well, for which they would trade lead from a "lead mine" whose location was unknown. William traded for lead for his use as musket balls, net or fishing weights or for trading with the logging camps.

Indians discovered Lead

William and the Indians would barter a deal, and the Indians would go to the "lead mine" and retrieve the amount of lead that they agreed on, bringing it back in chunks. My dad told me this story as a young boy, and I was mystified about the "lead deposit."

When I got to college, I took the mystery of the "lead deposit" to the Division of Geological Sciences at the University of Florida (even though I was attending FSU at the time) and was told that there could be no "lead deposit or mine" in that area of Florida.

Possible Shipwreck in Wacasassa

They suggested that since it was close to Wacasassa Bay, it was more likely that the Indians had discovered an old ship wreck, and what they were chopping out were chunks of pig lead ballast that would have remained on the marsh after the ship had rotted away.

The area was hit by hurricanes in October of 1842 that brought a storm surge of 27 feet and another in September of 1896 with a 10 foot surge that destroyed hundreds of boats in the sponge fleet that worked out of Cedar Key at that time.

The storms resulted in the center of the sponge industry moving from Cedar Key to Tarpon Springs, and the wood products port to Tampa, but that is another story!

They further theorized that the Indians may have found a lead fly-wheel of an abandoned steam or animal powered timber saw that was used to harvest the abundant hardwoods in Gulf Hammock.

When GPS came along, and the image quality improved in 2005, I searched the whole area zoomed in at the highest resolution, looking for anything that might resemble a ship wreck. I was so excited when I found what looked like horizontal beams of the bottom of a boat along with what appeared to be the ribs of a boat, in the dry creek bed of Dry Creek, which would be in the range that the Indians would have to walk to obtain the lead. After much study, I was sad to learn that it was an ATV bridge that was built when the area was turned into a Recreational Area some years ago.

The Watson Homesite

This place in Gulf Hammock, which became known as "the old Watson place," is where William Tell Watson, his wife Ardelar Curry lived with their son, Dewitt Talmadge Watson.

William and Ardelar divorced at some point, and Ardelar stayed on with son Talmadge until Talmadge took his wife, Gracie Tindale, and moved to Rosewood, working in the timber mill there.

After the "Rosewood Massacre," Talmadge and Gracie moved to a farm near Ellzey, Florida.

After Gracie's untimely death from an infection following childbirth in 1935, Talmadge took care of their 8 kids for a year, until he took another wife, Edith Smith. Talmadge and Edith later moved to Jacksonville, and the second Watson place soon was abandoned and eventually burned.

Dewitt   Eugene   Talmadge holding Doris   Ardella   Grace holding Robert   Murrel   Leon

Nothing of its structures still remains except for a pile of bricks that once was the chimney that was piled around a rose bush that was in the yard. The area has since been planted in pines.

The Watson Trail

While living at the "old Watson place," William and son Talmadge cut a trail to the Pat - Mac mainline railroad, and on through the hammock to each of the Pat - Mac logging camps in the area. The camps were named alphabetically, and the areas are still known as camps A-E over the vast area of the hammock. They followed the trail in horse and wagon loaded with grains, fruits, vegetables, other dry goods and meats to trade with the loggers in the camps.

After he left his boyhood home and moved to Ellzey, Talmadge cut the road on through close to his farm in Ellzey. The road became known as the Watson Trail, and continues to exist today. When this author was pastor of the Otter Creek Baptist Church, I remember well exploring the woods between Camp E and the marsh and I have vivid memories of the "Old Watson Place." There was nothing there but some bricks and the remains of an old windmill. Never did I dream that our families would later marry and we would have four generations of Keith/Watsons hunting and fishing in the same woods and waters. I want to thank Franklin, for this chapter of interesting information.

Chapter 23

The Watson, Gore, and Berryhill Families

This is Kyle Watson, who is married to Angela Robertson, who is the daughter of our daughter, Sandy (Keith) Robertson, who was born in Otter Creek.

As we mentioned earlier, three of our children, Sandy, Jimmy, and David, were born in Otter Creek.

Pioneer Levy County Families

At the present time, all but one of our children are now in some way related to, what I call, pioneer Levy County families. The Keith family is now related by marriage to the Yearty's, the Watson's, the Berryhill's, the Gore's, the William's, the Meek's, and the Goodbred's.

You may recall that it was Kyle's grandfather, Dewitt Senior and his brother Murrell Watson, who first took the author to the flats out of Wacassassa back in 1954.

This is Kyle's family in a picture taken sometime before "Granny" and Kyle's father, Dewitt Watson III, died. Kyle's wife, Angela is not seen here. She is probably the one taking the picture.

Kyle – Regina - Jeromy

Regina (Berryhill - Watson) Mills with some of her grandchildren.

Regina is related to both the Goodbred's, and the Berryhill's. Her mother was Annie Kate Goodbred who married Willie Berryhill.

It was Regina's parents, Willie and Annie Kate Berryhill who allowed us to build our own hunting camp on their property near the old Williams Fishcamp Landing.

The next picture was taken down at our camp near the gate to the Fiber Factory Hunt Club.

This is the son of Kyle and Angela, and the great grandson of Dewitt Watson Jr.

This was his fifth birthday party and he is seen by the fire holding his *lifetime hunting license*.

You can tell that he has Watson blood.

Chapter 24

The Yearty, Williams, and Walrath Families

This picture was taken years ago of our grandchildren at our hunting camp in Gulf Hammock. Several of them met their spouses there. Will Yearty and Michelle (Keith) Meeks are sitting on the Honda. Left to right standing are: Daniel Robertson, Troy Riviere, Amanda (Keith) Howe, Angela (Robertson) Watson, Rebekka (Keene) Wade, Steven Keith, and Liz (Keith) Yearty.

Sammy and Evelyn Yearty - Ginny (Yearty) Keith's Parents

The Keith family married into the Yearty family twice.

Billy Keith, the son of Pastor Bill and Vonnie Keith, married Ginny Yearty, the daughter of Sammy and Evelyn Yearty, seen in the picture above.

Liz Keith, the daughter of Bill and Vonnie Keith, married Will Yearty, the son of Danny and Charlotte Yearty.

Billy and Ginny (Yearty) Keith with Emma Grace and Little Will

Our grandson, "Little Billy" Keith, met his wife Ginny Yearty, at our old hunting camp in Gulf Hammock. Ginny (Yearty) Keith is the daughter of Sammy and Evelyn Yearty of Gulf Hammock.

Ginny is the Principal of the Creekside Christian School in Otter Creek and "Little Billy" is the pastor of the Rafter Cross Cowboy Church in Williston, Florida. Billy was recently appointed as the Director of Cowboy Churches in Florida and in Georgia.

The Rafter Cross Cowboy Church in Williston

Emma Grace Keith at a Rodeo

Ginny Yearty is the daughter of Evelyn Yearty who is the daughter of Burton Jay Walrath and Virginia (Delaino) Walrath of Cedar Key. Evelyn taught school in Cedar Key for 31 years and still teaches piano.

Evelyn with her father holding "Little Will."

Evelyn's Father was Burton Jay Walrath, Jr., who was 1st Sgt. in the 164th Combat Engineers. He landed on Omaha Beach, D-day +4, fought in France, Belgium and Germany in WWII.

Danny and Charlotte (Williams) Yearty, Will Yearty's Parents, in the famous Wekiva

As we mentioned earlier, the Keith family married into the Yearty family twice.

Billy Keith, the son of Pastor Bill and Vonnie Keith, married Ginny Yearty, the daughter of Sammy and Evelyn Yearty.

Liz Keith, the daughter of Bill and Vonnie Keith, married Will Yearty, the son of Danny and Charlotte Yearty.

Pictures of the Yearty Kids by Liz Yearty

They Love Sports

The Yearty kids enjoy fishing on the flats with their Mom and Grandfather, Bill Keith

Chapter 25

The Byrd Family

Bill and Vonnie Keith's youngest daughter, Lauren, married Jason Byrd of Gulf Hammock.

Jason and Granddaddy Byrd in the Parade

The Byrd Boys

The Byrd gang on the flats with their mom and their granddaddy, Bill Keith

The Byrd Gang Having Fun

Chapter 26

The Meeks Family

Rock and Michelle (Keith) Meeks and their precious family.

Stevie and Celeisa Keith – the parents of Michelle (Keith) Meeks. This picture was taken before little "Liza" was born.

The Meeks family is a legend in Levy County and hunting and fishing is in their blood. Rock Meeks is the founder and President of the North Florida Dog Hunting Association.

Mrs. Marie Meeks

Perhaps the best known and most loved Meeks in the history of Levy County was "Mrs. Marie." Marie was the first born child of eleven born to Waldo and Emily Gilley on February 13, 1920. She was married to Rufus "Coot" Meeks on September 19, 1931. "Mrs. Marie" taught school in Levy County for 33 ½ years. She taught Sunday school in the Ellzey United Methodist Church for 70 years.

She was my son Bill's first grade teacher when he attended "OCS" (Otter Creek Public School).

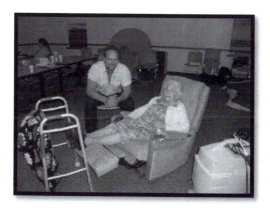

Doris Sheffield

The picture below is Rock Meeks' grandmother. Mrs. Doris Sheffield is a fourth generation Cedar Key native. Her mother had married an Indian and they both lived on a reservation near Ocala.

When Doris' grandfather died, Doris' mother was kicked off of the reservation because she was not a full blooded Indian. She then moved to Cedar Key and became a commercial fisherman. Mrs. Doris Sheffield still lives on her old home place in Cedar Key.

Rock's Parents - Russell and Mary Jane Meeks

Rock Meeks was elected to serve as a Levy County Commissioner on November 18, 2014

Chapter 27

The Haldeman, Baker, & Bishop Families

Our grandson, Jimbo, married Sarah Haldeman from Cedar Key. Sarah is a fifth generation Cedar Key girl.

Jimbo's Parents - Jimmy and Gwen Keith

Sarah's Parents - Gary and Dottie Haldeman

Sarah's grandmother was a Bishop, her grandfather was a Baker, and her father was a Haldeman from Pennsylvania.

Jimbo and Sarah's Children

Captain Jim Keith, who was born in Otter Creek, is the father of Captain Jimbo Keith. Both father and son have been fishing these waters all of their lives. This is Jimbo's son with his first snook caught in the Wacasassa River.

Captains Jimmy Keith, Jimbo Keith, Stevie Keith, Steven Keith, and Robbie Robertson are all fishing guides.

www.fishcedarkey.com

Chapter 28

Henry Strong: Great Grandson of a Slave

The Henry Strong family has a rich legacy in Levy County. Mr. Strong's Great Grandfather was a slave who helped build the railroad that once stretched from Fernandina on Florida's East Coast to Cedar Key on the West Coast.

Purchased Property

When Mr. Strong's grandfather won his freedom, his owner gave him $300 cash. His owner told him there was land for sale in a place east of Cedar Key known as "Cooter Slide" (now known as Otter Creek).

Henry's grandfather bought a large tract of property in Otter Creek and in, what is now the Wacasassa and McGee Branch hunting clubs. Henry told me (June 2013) that his grandfather paid 50 and 75 cents per acre for the land.

Henry was 84 years old when we talked and has passed away since then.

He served in Korea in the United States Army. Upon his return to Otter Creek, Henry hauled pulp wood for Lewis Renfroe.

He smiled as we talked, remembering he earned $2.50 per load back in those days. He said that on a good day he would haul eight loads and felt like he was rich at the end of the week.

Old Railroad Bed

The old railroad bed can still be seen on Main Street in Otter Creek, running East and West directly in front of the Otter Creek Baptist Church and the Creekside Christian School.

The following picture was taken looking south from the Otter Creek Baptist Church. The green grass between the two streets is what remains of the old railroad from Cedar Key to Fernandina, which was built by slaves.

100 Year Old Church

In the next picture, longtime Levy County resident, Sammy Yearty, is pictured here pointing to one of the oldest church buildings in Levy County.

This church is approximately 100 years old and is located in Otter Creek near the home of Henry Strong. The late Mrs. Henry Strong was the caretaker of this church building before her death.

This building is so rich in history it is a shame to allow it to deteriorate like this. My daughter, Sandy (Keith) Robertson is praying that perhaps some of us could purchase this building, restore it, and turn it into a historical site. Mr. Strong warned that vandals would soon destroy it if we did.

Chapter 29

The Gulf Hammock Community Church

Another site that is rich in Levy County history is the old Community Church building just West of US 19 in Gulf Hammock, Florida. This was a popular church back in the days when Gulf Hammock was thriving.

Gulf Hammock School

Pastor Peter Lord

A well-known pastor by the name of Peter Lord, was one of the early pastors of the Gulf Hammock church. Peter graduated from Bob Jones University, moved to Gulf Hammock and served as the pastor of this very church.

Pastor Sam Quincy

The late Pastor Sam Quincy, who at that time, served as pastor of the Ebeneezar Baptist Church near Trenton, baptized Peter Lord into the Baptist faith. After serving in Gulf Hammock, Peter moved to the First Baptist church of Bellview, Florida, where he served before moving to the Park Avenue Baptist Church in Titusville.

Gulf Hammock Community Church

Mission Sunday school

When I served as the pastor of the Otter Creek Baptist Church (1954-1959) we had a mission Sunday school in that very building. We would drive down at 9 o'clock every Sunday morning with several teachers and have a Bible study. On special occasions, like revivals, the young people met after school and had a youth choir practice.

Fleas in the Church

The dogs in Gulf Hammock loved that old church too. The doors were always open and it was cool inside. In the summer time, dogs would sleep all over the floor. The only problem was, the dogs brought fleas and they would bite us on our legs during Sunday school. However, that problem was not difficult to "fix."

The men would cut myrtle bushes and spread them all over the floor and the fleas would leave. This is the best cure for fleas we know of. *It always worked.*

Gulf Hammock School: Seventh & Eighth Grades (1947-1948?)

Picture provided by Zelda (Parnell) Lott

Front Row (Left to Right)

Billy Gore, Don Hummel, Ann Bond, Kay Parnell, Orine Osteen, Maxine Smallwood (Nurse Tommie's daughter), Iola Watson, and William Rosier.

Back Row (Left to Right)

Don Foley, Mary Lou Yearty, Hazel Fralix, J.T. Gallion, **Mr. Herman Guy Smith (Principal & Teacher)**, Bill Smallwood, Beck Blackburn, Carlene Jones, and Jasper Mashburn.

Chapter 30

Rosewood: What Hollywood Left Out

My information about Rosewood came from the oldest man in Levy County, who remembered vividly what happened back in January 1923.

A Black man from Sumner had been accused of raping a White woman.

Killed Deputy Wilkerson

A Deputy Sheriff named Wilkerson, and a Mr. Andrews, who owned the mill in Otter Creek, went to Rosewood to arrest the man who had been accused of rape. Deputy Wilkerson and Mr. Andrews were both shot dead while entering the house to apprehend the accused. This sparked the horrible things that followed.

Strangers descended on Rosewood

According to my source, who is 104 years old, most of the people involved in the violence *were not from Levy County*, but were from up in the Jacksonville area (Bradford or Union County), where Mr. Andrews had come from.

Protected Black Families

Another thing the movie didn't tell was that several White families protected the Black families from the violence.

Brothers Nick and Bert West who owned a turpentine still in Ellzey hid Black families in their barn where they gave them shelter, food, water, and safety.

Another man from Gulf Hammock, whom I knew well, hid some of his Black friends under his house until the crisis was over.

      I'm glad those days are behind us.

Chapter 31

A Redneck Wedding

Have you ever been to a *real* redneck wedding? You haven't lived until you do. One of the most enjoyable ones I ever performed was performed right there in Pastor Bill Keith's yard on the Wekiva.

Chester Smith and Mary gave their lives to Christ and were baptized. They already had a few kids and figured since, now that they were saved, it would be pleasing to God for them to get married.

They had just one request. They wanted to be married right there where they had been baptized.

Mary is the daughter of my friend, Booger Red, who lives up in Fairbanks. I will tell you about Booger in the book, "The Legend of Booger Red." But for now, let's get back to the wedding.

All went normal until I pronounced them "man and wife." No sooner had I uttered those words, when Chester's friends picked him up, removed his boots, and threw him into the creek.

Mary saw that and it scared her. *She broke and ran* towards the house. The men chased Mary down, picked her up, and threw her into the creek with Chester. We all had a good laugh and a great time. You haven't lived yet until you attend a Redneck Wedding.

Chapter 32

Bill's Otter Creek Memories

By Pastor Bill Keith

Our oldest son, Bill, was three years old when I became the pastor of the Otter Creek Baptist Church. He later became pastor of this same church and served as their pastor for 18 years.

This chapter includes his childhood memories of Otter Creek and Levy County.

The Smith Girls

One thing I remember from the first grade at Otter Creek School (OCS) was all the pretty girls there! I liked them a lot but really wasn't interested in settling down at that point, but I sure noticed how good they looked! I had decided to put marriage off for a while and pursue my cow-boying.

Gunsmoke was the rage right then and all I wanted to do was be able to draw my gun as fast as Matt Dillon did at the beginning of each episode on TV.

That Christmas I asked for and got a Mattel *"Fanner 50"* cap pistol with a quick draw holster so I could hone my skills. You can actually still buy them today on E-bay but they are a lot more expensive than they were back then. I'll tell you more about my "Fanner 50" and quick draw experience later.

Some of the young ladies that graced our school were, Betty Jo Standridge, Charlotte Williams, Erlene Williams, Aline Smith, Lois Smith, and a quite a few more. The Smith sisters were from Gulf Hammock and had two or three other sisters as well, and they all caught the eyes of the boys at school!

All the boys at OCS decided which of the girls at school they were going to marry, and told the other boys to leave them alone because they were already taken! It was kind of like an unwritten rule of the west, you didn't mess with another man's woman! The girls didn't know this was the rule, but it was there, none-the-less! The day was soon coming when I would have the whole bunch to myself, and the other boys wouldn't even be around!

My dad fished a lot out of the Wacasassa River and kept us supplied with plenty of fresh fish to eat. One day when he was fishing in the river the Smith brothers, R.V. and L.U. stopped to chat.

They had been catching *Florida Cooters* (Pseudemys Forida) in the river and were heading back in to clean them. (Everyone here called them **"Streaked Head Turtles**" or "Cooters").

They gave him three "streaked head" turtles from their day's catch, something my dad knew would be appreciated by my mom! *She would run you a "foot race" for any turtle, especially a "Soft Shell"!*

They then asked dad if he wanted to come over on Sunday afternoon and eat some fried cooter at R.V.'s house with them. Dad said, "Sure, we'll be there!"

When dad came home and told us about it I about shouted Hallelujah! Mr. R.V. was the father of those beautiful Smith girls! I could hardly wait! I would be able to be around them without all those other competitors!

Sunday came and we went to church as usual, but I had a hard time concentrating! I was thinking about going to the Smith girls' house and having some great food! Their mother, Mrs. Grace Smith was one of the best cooks around, especially with anything that was fried! I just knew it was going to be a very good day! We changed our clothes after church and headed to Gulf Hammock where they lived.

When we pulled up in the yard there was no vehicle in the yard, and no sign of the girls! In fact, there was no sign of anybody! They were gone!

In all the excitement of getting home just before evening, cleaning a mess of cooters, and consuming a few "*Miller High-Lifes,*" the men had forgotten to tell Mrs. Grace about their invitation to the preacher and his family for Sunday dinner! They had gone elsewhere that afternoon not realizing that a hungry herd of Keiths would soon be descending upon their home.

As we quietly turned around and headed back to Otter Creek, I was very disappointed at not having some of Mrs. Grace's fried turtle, but even more disappointed that I didn't get to see her daughters! That little event didn't change a thing about our family's friendship with their family. That was way back in 1957 and we have been good friends since then!

RV found the Lord

When I was Pastor at Otter Creek Baptist, 35 years later, Brian Crawford and I had the awesome privilege of leading Mr. R.V. to the Lord Jesus Christ in his home.

A year or so later we were with the Smith girls and their dear mother, Mrs. Grace, when Mr. R.V. left this earth for Heaven. The gospel songs that his sweet daughters were singing to him right before he left still resonate in my mind, songs of peace, comfort, and the Grace of God.

Those times always remind me of what the Bible says, "For whosoever shall call upon the Name of The Lord shall be saved."(Romans 10:13)

Mr. R.V. didn't get into Heaven because of his good works. He got into Heaven just like God said we could enter, by calling upon the Name of The Lord!

It also reminds me that we are all family. Although not blood kin, these wonderful friends from our past are truly family to us. But more than that, we are related through our faith in the God!

Ephesians 3:14 says, "For this cause I bow my knees unto the Father of our Lord Jesus Christ,

15 of whom the whole family in heaven and earth is named." We are kin, because of faith in Him!

If you want to be a part of our great big family, you can join too! Ask Jesus to be your Lord and Savior today! And who knows, you may get to meet my Smith sisters too!

My 22 Magnum

By Bill Keith

Shooting a .22 magnum rifle has to be one of the greatest of shooting experiences if you like shooting rifles. There is virtually no recoil on the powerful little rim fire round, but you get extended range and twice as much punch as a .22 long rifle. It is illegal in most states to hunt deer with a .22 magnum, although many still harvest deer with them. In the 1960s the .22 magnum was allowed when deer hunting.

The first time I hunted with my .22 magnum was right after Christmas in 1963. We were hunting on the fish camp road bed. It really was an extension of SR 326 in Gulf Hammock, Florida. The road bed was being carved through the woods and swamps west of highway 19 where it started, it then ended 3 miles to the west at the County Boat Ramp. There were no bridges across the creeks and sloughs at that point so we had to come to that particular hunting spot by boat.

My stand was on the curve where the old rail road tram entered the road bed. For some reason deer have always liked to cross right there, even until this day! I hadn't been there long when I saw deer crossing about 150 yards west of me. One of them looked like it might have horns so I shot a round at it. Of course, at that distance I didn't hit the moving target, but it was fun trying anyway!

When I went back to the boat dad asked me what I had shot at. I replied, "at a deer." He then asked me if it had horns. I replied that I thought it did! He reacted rather abruptly and warned me to never shoot again unless I was absolutely certain that it had horns! Dad was a real stickler for obeying the letter of the law! He would have made a great Game Warden!

As I was thinking about shooting at that deer without really knowing if it was a legal buck or not, I remembered the words of Paul to the Philippian Christians,

"Dear friends, you always followed my instructions when I was with you. And now that I am away, it is even more important. Work hard to show the results of your salvation, obeying God with deep reverence and fear." (Philippians 2:12) (NLT)

Dad taught us to obey the law even when he wasn't looking! He taught us self-control with regard to hunting and shooting. That was great character training for me and my brothers. We don't even think about breaking the law because we reverence what our father taught us! But more important than that is that we reverence and fear God! I wish more people did!

The Cotton Mouth

By Bill Keith

When the Fiber Factory was first opened to hunting around the 1966-67 hunting season it was a virgin tract of land that held a lot of great hunting.

The two main ponds that I remember were Mattie Pond, and Crab Pond. Although there were quite a few other ponds, sloughs, and tidal creeks in this tract of land, these two ponds were the largest and easiest ones to access.

Mattie Pond

Mattie Pond was loaded with nice bass! Some of the wives of our hunting group would take a small john boat in there and fish while we were all hunting. It was also a great place to duck hunt and would fill up with hundreds of ducks right before dark! Another spot in that area that held some great bass fishing was called the "smoke house" by those in the "know." But that's a story for another day!

Crab Pond

Crab Pond was somehow tied to the tidal creeks that crisscrossed the marsh land at the end of the Peninsula that was the Fiber Factory area. Crab pond lived up to its name by being full of large blue crabs!

This particular story happened when we were living down at Cape Canaveral and had come up to hunt for a few days. I was a teenager in the 10th or 11th grade at the time. As I walked into the woods off of the main tram I picked a dried up creek bed that looked like a good place for deer or hogs to cross through and walked along the edge looking for a good place to set up a stand. I walked along quietly, listening and watching to see any game that might get up ahead of me. I had learned that if you stop, look, and listen, you can move along almost silently through the woods.

On one of my pauses to stop, look, and listen, I thought I heard something. I stood there motionless for a couple of seconds, when something caused me to look down at my feet. There, no more than a few feet from my leg, was a humongous Moccasin all coiled up and ready to strike!

His large white mouth was wide open as if to say "I am going to bite you real good, you dumb old boy!"

Without moving a muscle in my legs I slowly aimed my shotgun at his head and with one blast of 00Buckshot ended his threat forever! He was almost 6 feet long and was as big around as my calf muscle! How I had almost walked over him without seeing him was a shock to me. I learned a valuable lesson that day, watch where you are putting your feet!

Life is so much like that isn't it? We concentrate so much on our progress and our activities in the world that we forget to watch out where our feet are walking and soon we step right into trouble! A little song I learned as a child sure did fit my situation that day.

"Oh be careful little feet where you go, O be careful little feet where you go, there's a Father up above, And He's looking down in love, so, be careful little feet where you go."

That little song also talks about what our eyes see, what our hands do, what we say with our mouths, and what we allow to enter our ears. All of those areas can lead us into danger if we are not careful!

The Bible calls Satan, our enemy, that old serpent, in Revelation 12:9.

"This great dragon—the ancient serpent called the devil, or Satan, the one deceiving the whole world—was thrown down to the earth with all his angels."

He's still alive and well and just waiting for unsuspecting humans to step on his coils! So, watch where you are walking.

Jungle Drums in the Night

By Bill Keith

You might remember this quote from the movie "The Wizard of Oz." Dorothy, Toto, the Scarecrow, and Tin Woodsman are traveling along the Yellow Brick Road when they come to a forest. She asks them if there are animals in the forest. They reply, "Probably a lot of lions and tigers and bears." They start skipping along, repeating that over and over. And, suddenly out of the forest comes a fierce lion, but he turns out to be the "Cowardly Lion", who is more frightened than they are!

I've often thought of that silly little scene from the Wizard of Oz, particularly when I'm walking to my deer stand alone, before daylight, tromping through palmettos, or ankle deep swamp water. I've never been eaten by a lion, tiger, or bear, yet! I have never even seen one of them while in the woods, but the thought has crossed my mind!

I know that's silly and unreasonable because we don't have lions or tigers in Florida woodlands, although we do have bears! The closest thing to a lion we have are our elusive Florida panthers. After having lived in, and hunted Florida woodlands for over 50 years I've only seen two of them in the wild, and they were quickly trying to run away and hide!

However, I have had a few close calls with rattlesnakes and moccasins that dwell in the swamps where I hunt.

When I was six or seven years old, living in Otter Creek, Florida, I had to learn to overcome fears that most children have at that age. One of those fears was fear of the darkness.

I don't know where the concept of the "boogie man" came from, but we all knew he was out there hiding, waiting for us to step out into the darkness so that he could grab us! Why we tormented each other with the "boogie man" I'll never know! It was fun, yet terrifying at the same time!

Within a half mile of where we lived was an African-American church. Their evening services lasted many times late into the night, or at least it seemed that way. There was no A/C in churches or most homes in those days in the mid 1950's. All windows had screens on them so the windows could remain open for air circulation. The night sounds would serenade us to sleep each evening.

About the time bedtime came for the children in the Keith household, the African-American church would just be getting warmed up! We couldn't hear the words or songs from that distance, but we could hear their big bass drum! It sounded to us just like the Tarzan movies of that era.

As we lay there in the darkness listening to those drum beats we could picture a big campfire with a caldron full of hunters and explorers tied up and piled in it. We could picture the natives dancing around them getting ready for their evening meal!

And all the while there was that ole "boogie man", peeking in our window, or so we thought, to add to the terror!

It was scary to small children who didn't know all the facts! Those were unrealistic fears produced by our minds...yet they seemed very real at the time!

As I studied the Scriptures, one became my favorite during scary times! I learned this Scripture in public school in the first grade. Psalm 23:1-6

"The Lord is my shepherd; I shall not want. He maketh me to lie down in green pastures:

He leadeth me beside the still waters.

He restoreth my soul: he leadeth me in the paths of righteousness for his name's sake.

Yea, though I walk through the valley of the shadow of death, I will fear no evil: for thou art with me; thy rod and thy staff they comfort me.

Thou preparest a table before me in the presence of mine enemies: thou anointest my head with oil; my cup runneth over.

Surely goodness and mercy shall follow me all the days of my life: and I will dwell in the house of the Lord forever."

As I grew out of my childhood fears, I did it as I learned to trust in the God of the Bible. I have found that there are very few things that actually cause fear now. Why? Because I trust in the God who cares, and I know that He does not cause crippling fear!

When I do have fear, I stop and put my trust back in the God who cares! Psalm 56:3 *"But when I am afraid, I will put my trust in you."* (NLT)

His Word promises us this: 2 Timothy 1:7 "For God hath not given us the spirit of fear; but of power, and of love, and of a sound mind."

One thing I know for sure! The God of the Bible doesn't want us to live in fear! He promised us this in Isaiah 26:3 *"You will keep in perfect peace all who trust in you, all whose thoughts are fixed on you!"* (NLT)

If you are like Dorothy today and you are going through life fearful about what could happen, stop! Put your trust in the God of the Bible! He promises to keep you safe!

Momma! There's a Bear in our Yard!

By Bill Keith

During part of my life in Otter Creek as a small boy, this experience shaped my destiny as having "bear-a-phobia."

It was late one Sunday afternoon, right at dusk. The parsonage we lived in was only a few hundred yards from the Otter Creek Baptist Church where my father pastored at the time.

I was feeling my oats at the ripe old age of 6 or 7 and decided I wanted to walk by myself to church, to which my mother agreed. I knew I mustn't miss "Training Union" as it was called in those days! I mostly wanted to get there to play with my buddies, Mike Meeks and Danny Yearty. We still don't know what the training was all about, but it was expected, so we went! And evidently we did learn a few things that would later help us!

There was a wooded path that cut through a little patch of woods between the road we lived on and Third Street where the church was. The trees and brush formed a tunnel across this little path, making it a little dark and foreboding as the sun slipped behind the trees to the west. As I neared this critical part of my 200 yard solo journey to church, I saw something coming toward me that caused the hair to suddenly stand up on the back of my neck!

I froze in terror for one millionth of a second, then turned and ran back home screaming in terror! Coming down that path was a big old black bear lumbering toward our house!

I ran through the front door, slamming it shut as I entered! Frantically, I screamed *BEAR, there's a BEAR coming down the path!* I began closing and locking every window I could, knowing this "man-eating" bear was right on my tail!

My mom looked out the side window and began to laugh! By now the "bear" had emerged from the tunnel of terror and came out into the last rays of fleeting sunlight so you could really see him in all his majesty!

Mom said, "*Billy, that's not a bear!*" "*That's just old Slim pushing his wheel barrow!*" I took another look and sure enough, it was old Slim, the kind old black man that lived nearby. It was a rather cool evening for Florida, and slim had on an old dark "*Navy P coat.*" He was humped over his loaded-down wheel barrow which was filled with hay for Mrs. Ruby West's cows that were in her pasture just across the road from our house and next door to the Otter Creek School.

I felt silly! But the fear was real! I really thought I saw a large black bear! From that time on I kept my eye open for bears as I traveled that toilsome path to church and back! Within a short time I would have to "test-my-metal" against a bear that attacked my younger sister, but that's a story for another day!

Our fears are a lot like that. We tend to over react to things that cause us to flee or panic, when in reality there is nothing there to fear! We get ourselves in more trouble when we panic and lose our ability to think clearly. I'm thankful to have had parents that helped me overcome many of the things that caused fear in me as a small child.

Here are some of the wonderful Bible verses I learned in Training Union those many years go, and from my parents, that helped me overcome the fears I had. I hope they comfort and strengthen you as well when you are confronted with "bears" or other frightful things!

Psalm 23:4 "Yea, though I walk through the valley of the shadow of death, I will fear no evil: for thou art with me; thy rod and thy staff they comfort me."

Psalm 27:1 "The Lord is my light and my salvation; whom shall I fear? "

Psalm 27:3 "Though a mighty army surrounds me, my heart will not be afraid. Even if I am attacked, I will remain confident."(NLT)

Psalm 34:4 "I sought the Lord, and he heard me, and delivered me from all my fears."

The Day I Fought the Bear

By Bill Keith

The day I faced my fear of bears started like a normal day in the sleepy little hamlet of Otter Creek, Florida. Nestled in the piney woods of north central Florida, Otter Creek is situated at the crossroads of SR 24 which runs east and west, and Highway 19 which runs north and south.

Otter creek is located directly in the center of Levy County, and served as the county seat years ago before it was moved to Bronson.

In the 1920s and 1930s Otter Creek boasted a population of over 1,000 and was the second largest city in Levy County. Now the population hovers around 130 on any given year. 3-4 miles south of Otter Creek on highway 19 is a bridge where the Wacasassa River crosses as it winds toward the Gulf of Mexico 6-7 miles to the west.

Back in the days of my childhood there was a general store next to the bridge called Mack Hodge's Store. It seems I remember them selling gas as well. The store was a marvelous place to go and hang out or pick up pretty much anything one would need to hunt, fish, cook, or eat as they passed by that way. Mack Hodges was the local

Game Warden as well, serving the ancient hunting grounds called Gulf Hammock. The Buck Island Grade (road) entered the Gulf Hammock land management area right beside this neat old country store.

This particular day my parents had stopped at Mack Hodges' station to pick up some sort of food or supplies. What I remember most was being there with my parents and my little sister, Sissy. This was before the population explosion caught up with my mom and dad.

My little sister wandered around the side of the store nearest the river. As I rounded the corner of the store in pursuit of Sissy I saw the most terrifying sight I can remember up to that point! **There was a bear!**

And worse than that, he had my little sister! He was reared up on his hind legs over my little sister wrapping his front paws around her, and holding her down!

Without a thought I sprang into action! I ran up to that hairy beast and climbed up on his back grabbing his neck and head to pull him off of Sissy! It startled him so that he released Sissy and immediately turned his attention to me!

There I was with my arms wrapped around the back of a bear! I lost my grip on him as he spun around to see what had attacked him from behind. And there, in an instant I came face-to-face with my worst fear, that of a bear!

Sissy now rescued, I could now concentrate on teaching this wicked beast a thing or two about messing with my sister! He was getting ready to receive an old fashioned,

Otter Creek "*butt-whippin!*" I could smell his nasty breath as we squared off, face-to-face! We sized each other up as we circled, trying to see who would pounce first! I was so close to him I could smell his breath! It reeked with the smell of freshly chewed M & M's and other fine chocolates that the patrons that visited Mack Hodges would feed him when they would visit. I then saw my chance! I ran and escaped to the edge of the covered porch where his chain wouldn't reach! Mack Hodge's pet baby bear had sure helped me overcome my fear of bears!

What are you afraid of today? There are real things that cause real fear in our lives. If we trust in the God of the Bible, He will come to our aid when we have to face them. Psalm 118:6 "*The Lord is on my side; I will not fear: what can man do unto me?*" (KJV)

Psalm 56:4 "I praise God for what he has promised. I trust in God, so why should I be afraid? What can mere mortals do to me?" (NLT)

My parents taught me at a young age to overcome my fears. Many times I learned this through confronting my fears, as I did when I really believed that little bear was hurting my sister. He looked huge to me! I didn't know at the time that he was just playing and wasn't hurting her at all, but I didn't hesitate in attacking what I thought was a threat to Sissy! God used that situation on my life to teach me to attack my fears head-on! You can too with God's help and strength!

Psalm 18:29 "In your strength I can crush an army; with my God I can scale any wall."(NLT)

"Sissy! Stop Eating the Bait!"

By Bill Keith

We were hungry little youngsters when living in Otter Creek back in the 1950s. There were none of the "all-you-can-eat" buffets back then! Had there been one, we would not have been able to afford to eat there anyway!

Raising five children on a tight budget was pretty hard, but mom and dad always managed to provide. We never went to bed hungry or anything like that, but if there was anything edible around, we would consume it without delay! I'm not sure if the reason was we didn't eat enough of the right things, or maybe we had a vitamin deficiency, but we were always willing and able to eat anything that was offered. Now that I have five young grandsons and try to fill them up when they come over, I am starting to understand that we were not abnormal at all! We were just little kids who liked to eat!

My dad started fishing on the "flats" out in Wacasassa Bay soon after we moved to Otter Creek. The "flats" are the shallow grass waters that extend from the shore out about 6 or 7 miles into the Gulf of Mexico on Florida's west coast. The depth is very shallow, only dropping in depth a foot per mile, with the average depth around about 3-4 feet for miles!

The "flats" offer some of the best Speckled Trout (Cynoscion Nebulosus) in the state! In that day there was no limit on how many you could keep but they had to be at least 12 inches in length. Having grown up on the coast in Tarpon Springs, dad knew about Speckled Trout and a little on how to catch them. But, soon he would learn from the Watson brothers a much more effective way to harvest those great tasting specks!

Dewitt & Murrell Watson were two brothers that had been raised as small children deep in the woods of the Hammock. The "Watson Trail" that still exists as a graded road in the Hammock to this day, bears their family name. This was the road their father had cut through the Hammock some 80 years ago. The family home place was out near the "salt marsh" deep in Gulf Hammock.

The Watson brothers taught my dad the basics of fishing the bountiful flats of Wacasassa Bay. Another new found friend, Russell Goodbred, spent more time with dad helping him perfect his skill at catching trout. Ralph Green was a fishing guide down there and he taught dad how to troll for redfish with a River Runt lure.

Mr. Goodbred lived near the fish camp in Gulf Hammock and was a gillnet fisherman that knew the waters of the bay like the back of his hand. Many times he would yodel while netting for the fat mullet that thrived in the creeks around the bay. We'd be fishing out further in the flats and would hear that beautiful sound as it echoed across the

Gulf. Dad would say, "That's Mr. Goodbred catching mullet."

The Watsons grew up fishing the flats along with the Goodbreds and a few other families. Their fishing style was unlike anything my dad had ever seen! They would use an 18-20 foot cane pole, with a stout line on it.

The line was almost as long as the pole, with a long shank hook and a cork attached 2-3 feet from the end. Their bait was caught right there on the flats where they fished.

The bait was a small pin fish called a "shiner" by the locals, while fishermen on the east coast called them, "Sailor's Choice." The little fish would be cut in half across the middle and then the portion with the tail would be split in two. You would end up with two baits per pinfish. You would attach one of the "shiner tails" to your hook and then begin fishing. This is where the story takes a unique turn! Trout like a lot of noise and movement on the water, especially on top of the water!

The long pole was used to beat the top of the water to attract the trout. Later "popper corks" came into being and helped make the noise to bring the fish up.

In today's bait industry the newest cork we use is called the "Cajun Thunder." It is especially built with noise-making beads that attract most fish in the Gulf.

The trout come up to investigate the noise being made on top, thinking maybe other fish were striking minnows or shrimp. They then spot the freshly cut shiner tail and bite it! They would then be swung into the boat and into the cooler! It didn't take long to "load-the-boat" with fat speckled trout like that!

Our whole family would go trout fishing with dad on the flats. He taught us to fish like the Watson brothers had taught him. When dad would catch a shiner and cut it for bait, he would put the extra shiner tail on the bait board for the next one of us that needed a bait, and then he would turn and start fishing again.

In a few minutes he looked around to get the other bait, but it was gone! He would catch to or three of them, and repeat the process. He put a bait on his line and leave the extra ones on the bait board.

He decided to find out where all the bait was going. Watching out of the corner of his eye he soon saw Sissy's little hand grab the bait and quickly eat it! This had gone on for a while and now the mystery was solved! Sissy was eating our bait!

We didn't know it back then, but she was really way ahead of her time! Sissy liked Sushi! In fact, she was the first person in Levy county to eat it that we know of! The solution was found when mom and dad moved the bait up where she couldn't reach it!

Dad and mom had to watch her pretty close after that! They were afraid she'd get a bone or fin stuck in her little throat! If that happened we'd sure be in a mess due to how far we were from a hospital. So they just monitored her a little better.

Sensing that maybe it was time for Dinner (lunch for you Yankees out there) Mom would break out her stash of "health foods" like Vienna sausages, pork-and-beans, saltine crackers, RC colas, and best of all, "Moon Pies!" Soon we all were content and full, and Sissy would now leave the bait alone! In a short while the little ones would fall asleep up under the front deck, the wind would gently cool us off, and dad's little boat would gently rock our cares away. As the sun would start sinking into the Gulf and the day began to fade, dad would point that little boat back up river and we would soon be home. The old saying, "Home is where the heart is" is so true. Those days on the Gulf together fifty years ago still feel just like home to me!

Mom and dad never spanked or scolded my sweet little sister for her penchant for raw fish. They just loved her anyway and taught her to cook her fish before she consumed them!

They also taught us to live off the land by teaching us how to fish and hunt. These times together so long ago are etched into my mind as a beautiful tapestry of family togetherness and bonding. I'm thankful that I had parents who obeyed God by bringing children into this world and teaching them about the fish and animals that dwell here.

The Bible tells us that we are supposed to do this in Genesis 1:27-28 "So God created human beings in his own image. In the image of God he created them. Male and female he created them. Then God blessed them and said, "Be fruitful and multiply. Fill the earth and govern it. Reign over the fish in the sea, the birds in the sky, and all the animals that scurry along the ground." (NLT)

Chapter 33

The Miracle on Main Street
(Actually Third Street)

I may be a bit biased, but in my personal opinion, the most important thing to happen in Otter Creek in my lifetime was the establishment of the Creekside Christian School.

Our son, Bill attended the old Otter Creek Public School (now the Lark building) when he was a child. In those days the school only went to the sixth grade. After that all of the students were bused to Bronson.

Bill became the pastor of the Otter Creek Church and had a vision for a truly Christian School. After much prayer, hard work, and perseverance, the church opened a brand new school with grades K through 12. The school is still going strong and our granddaughter, Mrs. Ginny (Yearty) Keith serves as the Principal. Let's let Bill tell the story.

A History of the Creekside Christian School

By Bill Keith

My first church experience of church and hearing the sweet stories of Jesus was at Otter Creek Baptist Church. I remember Sunday school there as a small child of three or four with kind ladies teaching me about Jesus and the other great Bible heroes!

It wasn't hard for me to come back there 35 years later and become the pastor of that wonderful little church on the edge of the wilderness that is Gulf Hammock. Some of those kind ladies were still alive when my wife and I arrived back home there in 1992.

Little did we know at the time, but God had great plans in store for this out-of-the-way church on the edge of nowhere!

I attended public school for the first two years of my education at the Otter Creek (public) School that held classes for the first through sixth grades.

The old school closed after the integration of the 1960s. It was reopened sometime in the late 70s for a day training center for the Levy Association of Retarded Citizens and is still in operation as such to this day. The old building still brings back good memories of my childhood when starting school there so long ago.

I never planned to move back to Otter Creek and become the Pastor of the church there as I was very busy in ministry in my home church, the Countryside Baptist in Gainesville.

The opportunity came to me while on a hunting trip down in that area during the fall of 1992. Sammy Yearty, a family friend who was also chairman of the Deacon board there at Otter Creek Baptist, approached me as I was leaving the hunting woods one Saturday afternoon and heading home. He asked if I would pray about coming down and serving as their interim pastor until they could call a full time one. I told him that I would certainly pray about that.

I was then serving as the Principal of Countryside Christian School, as well as Visitation pastor, Staff Counselor, Song Leader, and Sunday school teacher for the Countryside Baptist Church where my father served as Senior Pastor.

I brought the idea before the men of Countryside and they agreed that God was leading me in that direction.

I accepted the call to serve as an interim pastor of Otter Creek, but still serve as Principal at Countryside Christian School.

This arrangement worked out well as I would travel over to Otter Creek on Wednesday nights and Sundays for church. We were living in Newberry at the time. It soon became evident that God had bigger plans for me at Otter Creek and soon they issued me the opportunity to become their full time Pastor, while still maintaining my other ministry as principal at Countryside. We were offered the use of the pastorium at Otter Creek as part of our salary there and agreed to move there.

Reluctantly we left our huge, beautiful 4 BR, 3 bath block home on five acres and moved into a small two bedroom one bath parsonage in Otter Creek. I had lived in this same small home as a young child when my father served as pastor there from 1954-1959. It hadn't changed much since that time and was quite a culture shock to my wife and children! But God had sent us there and that was where we were going to serve!

There were many children in the Otter Creek Church and the surrounding community at the time and I soon became burdened for them as I noticed how much illiteracy abounded among their numbers! Many of them were struggling with basic reading and writing and were already in the fourth and fifth grades in the public schools there. I knew that we had the answer for this, having served as a principal for five years in a Christian School before arriving.

I shared my burden with any that would listen and determined then and there to do my part to help them. I enlisted the best reading teacher we had at the time working at the Countryside Christian School. Mrs. Carole Bixby would come over on Wednesday nights and offer basic reading classes. We soon had five or six students on a regular basis with even a few adults coming to learn how to read.

Mrs. Bixby enlisted the help of her son Dale, one of our Countryside students, to come and tutor the students as well and soon many of them were making startling improvement in their reading ability! The miracle began as a Wednesday night reading class that helped plant the seeds and plow the ground that would a few years later grow into an even greater miracle!

God began to establish a clear vision of a Christian school there at Otter Creek during these humble attempts at helping these youngsters and a few adults learn to read. I knew that a school was what the church needed and began to share the vision with others.

Many Christians there caught the vision and began to change the way they viewed education, while others just wrote me off as a nut!

But, God wouldn't let me forget what He wanted done there and continued to inspire my mind with the idea and plan for a Christian school at Otter Creek.

I ate it, drank it, preached it, sold it, and did everything in my power to push toward starting a school there.

Finally on Sept. 24, 1996, (my birthday), during a Sunday night business meeting we voted about starting a school there. The vote ended with 51% in favor and 49% against.

We won the vote! Yet I felt in my heart of hearts that we should table the idea for a while and allow God to change the hearts of the other 49% before we pushed something through that might split that wonderful little church.

Many of the supporters were disappointed but understood that the idea and vision was correct, the timing was just not quite there yet! So we waited on God and continued winning people to Christ and building people in the faith.

I put the school idea on a back burner and quit even talking about it, knowing that God was more than able to move in the hearts and minds of the people when He was ready!

My youngest daughter was the last of my three children to graduate from Countryside Christian. She finished in May of 2001. I decided that it was time to retire from being a bi-vocational pastor and devote more time to building the church there at Otter Creek.

I resigned as Principal that summer and looked forward to resting a while with just one profession and calling. I certainly wouldn't miss the 83 mile round trip every day! Little did I know that my rest would be short-lived and God would push us forward into a great miracle!

It was then that the vision of a school at Otter Creek came rushing back to me from the Lord!

This time it came in the form of many of the leaders there at Otter Creek asking me when we were going to start "our school!"

The vision had grown from being something that only I was seeing to one that was embraced, cherished, and pushed by many of those I had ministered to for nine years!

God had been working overtime on pushing His agenda even when I had quit speaking much about it! I was in awe of how He had done these things and the Scripture from Acts 2:17 came to mind,

"And it shall come to pass in the last days, saith God, I will pour out of my Spirit upon all flesh: and your sons and your daughters shall prophesy, and your young men shall see visions, and your old men shall dream dreams:"

Some of the young people would share with me what God was saying to them about a school. An older man there told me he had seen in a dream the school with the parking lot already partially finished! I knew then it was time to pursue the dream again!

We held a business meeting and voted the second time on whether or not to start a school there. The vote was 99% in favor. There was only one vote against! The one that cast the nay vote was older and many thought that she didn't understand what we were even voting for!

The church fathers were still a little reluctant to take on a financial responsibility like that so it was agreed that they would allow Countryside Baptist Church to license the school and operate it there at the Otter Creek Baptist facility.

It was a partnership made in Heaven! We had the expertise on how to do it, we just needed a place to do it! Now we had that, and we made plans to open Creekside Christian School in the fall of 2001 in Otter Creek, Florida!

It was a marriage made in Heaven with two churches working together to establish something there that had never happened before! It was the miracle on Main Street!

I knew that Countryside didn't have the money to fund another school, but they did have the name and backing to stand behind this new school! So I set about the task of raising the necessary $5000-$6000 startup funds I knew we would need!

I had bought a large industrial planing machine quite by accident the year before this as a personal investment. I put a ridiculous bid of $50 on this machinery knowing that I would never get it for that price! Yet when the bids were tallied, the winning bid didn't fulfill his bid and I got the machine for $50! I immediately began to try and resell it thinking that perhaps it would provide some much needed cash for the Keith household!

It didn't sell for a long time! I advertised it all over the world on the internet, but to no avail! During the summer of 2001 a wood working shop opened in Otter Creek, 100 yards from our church door. The owner took one look at my big old machine and bought it instantly for $2,500!

I jumped up and down for joy thinking how awesome God was selling that stupid machine 100 yards from where He wanted the money used! Wow! What a sense of humor our God has!!

I wrote many of my friends and family members and asked them to help! They came through in such a miraculous way and soon we had enough seed money to start the school. We still needed desks and equipment and I begin to search for those things.

A school down in Titusville had closed part of their learning centers and had enough desks and much of the curriculum that we would need to begin our school. I offered them $2500 for all of it and they took it! A group of wonderful men with three trucks and trailers went with me there and we brought it all back to Otter Creek the same day! We immediately began setting up the learning center and classrooms and soon our little school was within a few weeks of starting!

Over those few months in the summer of 2001, we raised somewhere close to $10,000 in startup funding through the kindness and generosity of God's people. Some were kind enough to loan us funds over the first 5 or 6 years of the school there that made it possible to never have to ask for money or borrow from lending institutions of any kind! We were able to pay them back completely over the years and were never in debt as an institution!

Since that time, Creekside has experienced miracle after miracle as God provided for each and everything we would ever need to build and maintain a school! Starting with just 24 students and a vision from God we were able to establish a Christian School in Otter Creek that is still operating today. The student count now averages 60-70 each year and hundreds of boys and girls have been educated there.

Countless souls have been reached for the Kingdom of God through the efforts of the dedicated teachers and staff there at Creekside.

Although God called me back to my former mission at Countryside in 2010, the ministry there at Otter Creek still has a wonderful place in my heart! I am thankful for having been one of those that God used to help establish what He wanted there. Part of my family still serves there and my grandchildren are still attending school there. An added blessing is that I still get to conduct chapel in Otter Creek every Monday morning.

I hope and pray that the ministry of Otter Creek Baptist Church and Creekside Christian School is still in operation when the Lord returns one day for His church!!

Chapter 34

The Hurricane from Hell

By Bill Keith

Having grown up in Florida I have always known the danger and strength of Hurricanes. When I was a young boy a Category 5 hurricane, named "Donna" ripped up the length of Florida leaving massive damage and flooding all over our low-lying state.

Although only 10th in the list of costliest Atlantic hurricanes, Donna made a distinct impression on me as an 8 year old boy! I learned that hurricanes were not something to play with. When the warnings are issued by the Hurricane Center they are for real!

Although there have been some really devastating hurricanes to hit the US since then, Donna was my first! Many times first impressions set the tone for action throughout your life. Donna did that for me! There is nothing like the experience for a teacher!

"Throughout the state, the storm destroyed 2,156 homes and trailers, severely damaged 3,903, and inflicted minor impact on 30,524 others.

Approximately 391 farm buildings were destroyed, an additional 989 suffered extensive impact, and 2,499 others received minor damage.

Roughly 174 buildings were demolished, 1,029 received major impact, and 4,254 suffered minor damage. Additionally, 281 boats were destroyed or severely damaged.

A total of 50% of the grapefruit crop was lost, 10% of the orange and tangerine crops were ruined, and the avocado crop was almost completely destroyed. With at least $350 million in damage in Florida alone, Donna was the costliest hurricane to impact the state, at the time.

Additionally, there were 13 confirmed fatalities, six from drowning, four from heart attacks, two from automobile accidents, and two from electrocution. About 1,188 others were injured. (http://en.wikipedia.org/wiki/Hurricane_Donna)

Later when I was Pastor at Otter Creek Baptist in 2004, a Category 4 hurricane named "Charlie" made landfall at Port Charlotte on Florida's lower southwest coast, destroying most of the little towns in that area as it crossed Florida.

There was widespread destruction of the power grid as well from all the downed electrical towers and lines. What was significant about Charlie was that by this time the

Southern Baptist Convention had Disaster Teams in place that rushed to the area to aid other rescue organizations. (http://www.namb.net/dr/)

The Harmony Baptist Association, of which Otter Creek Baptist is a part, also has their own team that coordinated with the other Florida Baptist groups which all mobilized and went to the area to assist in the recovery.

I remember one Wednesday evening in church right after our teams had gone to the Port Charlotte area to lend disaster aid to the people. One of our members that had gone reported back to us that there were many churches that had closed their doors and posted "keep out" signs to warn off would be looters or the desperate hurricane victims. He then told of numerous Southern Baptist Churches that had opened up their churches as aid stations to help the hurricane victims find food and shelter.

I remember encouraging our people to never close their doors in the event of a catastrophe like that! We prayed that night that God would use us to help in the event something like that ever happening in our area. Little did we know that within a very short time God would answer our prayers.

Hurricane Frances

As Hurricane Frances started bearing down on Florida near the end of August I felt pressed in my spirit to do something I had never done. I felt that God was telling me to board up our church windows and prepare for moving my family and others there for protection from the approaching storm.

I conveyed my concern to others who helped me put plywood over all the windows and sandbag all the doors in case of flooding.

We Left Our Home

I have lived in Florida all my life and have never experienced what we were living through with these back-to-back Hurricanes from hell! There were a few times when we had to tape up our windows and it rained for numerous days, but nothing like this!

We live on the banks of a beautiful clear river in Levy County and knew from experience that the little river was probably going to flood. It was kind of expected, yet we didn't anticipate the mile long graded road that connected us to the highway and civilization to be covered with 2-3 feet of water in many places!

A couple of days before the storm came and the severe flooding commenced was when I was so impressed by the

Lord to start making preparations to move to the church on higher ground! I am so glad I listened!

I remember loading our vehicles with all the important personal things that we could pack in plastic containers. We packed things like our wedding pictures, pictures of our children, clothing, toiletries, food, wading boots, rain gear, and my guns.

We then moved our car and trucks to the church, 7 miles away. I remember the foreboding feeling that I had when we left our home that day, all boarded up and battened down. I thought to myself that only God can protect our little home now! My wife and I paused for prayer on our front porch and prayed for God's protection over the home that He had provided for us there.

We reminisced to Him all the times we had given it back to Him when we had held baptisms and church parties on the creek, in our yard and home.

A little plaque next to our front door reads, "*Bless This House O Lord We Pray, "Keep it safe by night and day"*. We both prayed that God would somehow protect our earthly dwelling during the coming storm. Little did we know that we would not live there again for three weeks!

We Were Ready

By the 5th of September, Hurricane Frances began her destruction of Florida. But we were ready. We had boarded up our home and moved to the church to prepare for those that would need us when the hurricane came through.

We were in for a shock as the hurricane knocked out power in our whole area, *except for our church,* for a couple of weeks! There was widespread damage to homes and buildings of our county.

We had as many as 65-70 people living and sleeping at the church for at least a week or two during and after that storm!

We were cooking 3-4 meals a day to feed them as well as many that came in from the area to eat a hot meal with us. We were feeding as many as 150 people per day!

All the freezers people kept their food in were useless with no power, so they brought their frozen foods and donated them to help feed the people.

There were many more that came at meal time, but stayed in their own homes at night! We had people sleeping in every nook and cranny of the church. Most of those that came were church members or residents of Otter Creek.

Quite a few were aged people who lived alone and had no electricity due to the lines being down. Some were completely un-churched until this point. This provided a great time to get to know people that had never darkened the door of the little church until now. Many opened up to our ministry after that and some came to know Christ as their Savior for the very first time!

The Emergency Management Director from our county called and told me that they couldn't authorize us as a shelter. I replied that we weren't under their authority and that God had already authorized us to minister to people, especially when they were in a situation where their homes were damaged or without power. I was nice and polite to him and asked him where I should send all these people since all the other shelters in the area were filled!

I also told him all the preparations we had made and how strong and dry our buildings were.

He then relented and became very helpful, knowing that we were for real and going to be there for the duration of the emergency! He replied we needed to keep doing what we were doing and that they would be sending us emergency rations and water soon!

By the next day the large trucks arrived full of MREs (Military Ready to Eat packages) and bottled water.

We were designated as one of the distribution points for the emergency food and water that FEMA was sending to our State. One whole end of our fellowship hall was stacked with bottled water and MREs!

Each citizen would be allowed a case of water and a box of MREs every two days or so depending on how many were in their family.

The Red Cross also gave us bags with emergency toiletries and supplies for each family.

We were also able to put a Bible in every bag along with a tract about Jesus! In all we distributed 2,000-3,000 MRE meals along with 200-300 cases of water or more! It was hard to calculate how much due to the crowds from all over the county and beyond, coming there to get their allotted food!

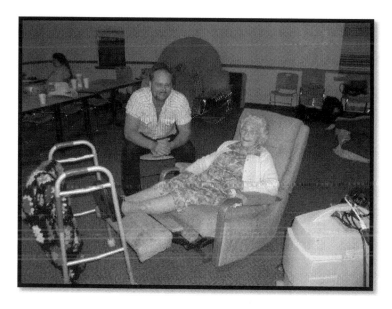

As we worked with the distribution of the food and water, supervising those that were staying there, and ministering to the crowds that came to our little church in the middle-of-nowhere,

I remembered our prayer only a couple of weeks earlier about God using us to minister should an emergency ever come there! God was certainly doing more than any of us ever dreamed we would be doing out of Otter Creek Baptist Church. And the amazing thing was that it was just starting!

God sure uses unlikely candidates to get the job done in emergency situations! We were right in the middle of meeting the needs of hundreds upon hundreds of the suffering citizens of our county.

We were also blessed to live in America where the food and water was free to all who came! Yet they ended up having to come to a little church in the middle of nowhere to get their food and water from us. We never dreamed that God would use us in such a wonderful way! It was an awesome time!

God Supplied Hot Food

The crowd at the church was very small to begin with because many residents thought this was an ordinary drill like we had always experienced when a hurricane passed through.

The church is right in the middle of the little town of Otter Creek, a small community of 130 or so residents. By the time that the power in most of our area was knocked out, many began to migrate to the church or to other shelters, all of which were 10-15 miles away.

During the whole ordeal the power was never out in Otter Creek except for 8 hours during that 3 week period! The Nextel cell tower nearby never lost service either. We were blessed to have cell service, internet, and electricity that never went down as it did in many places along our coast! This would prove very valuable in keeping up with the storm and communicating with the Emergency Management Team in Bronson, 11 miles away.

We also had a back-up generator in place that would operate the lights if needed. It wasn't large enough to run the whole church plant, yet it would at least provide lighting if needed.

We had plenty of food for the first few days, although feeding 75-150 people three meals a day can surely dwindle your supplies in a hurry!

Many of the residents that lived nearby were flooded out of their homes or had no electricity and ended up coming to stay with us at the church. I was particularly glad that some of the elderly in the area came too!

Some of them at risk with breathing problems and needed the electricity for machines and heat. Although it was early September it got rather cold with rain falling for a couple of weeks continually.

We prayed and asked God to provide more food for the crowds we were ministering to. The answer came immediately when the Southern Baptist Feeding Unit that had set up in Bronson started sending us hot meals two times a day. We were so thankful for the sudden answer to our prayers!

That lasted for about a week and then as the brunt of the storm approached they had to withdraw the feeding units to safer quarters until after the storm passed.

We prayed again that God would provide and the Red Cross began bringing hot meals twice daily. We were not only feeding those that were staying there, but also many of the residents that chose to stay in their homes, as well as the rescue workers in the area. The meal count was in the 150's for each meal! After a week the Red Cross pulled back and the incoming meals ceased once again, but only for a little while.

We Prayed a Third Time

We prayed a third time asking God to provide. The phone rang and someone at Central Florida Electric Coop called asking if we could use hot food there! Could we? We replied yes!

They had 250 electrical workers from all over the country there to help repair all the downed power lines. They were cooking for them daily and had tons of food left over for each meal.

They soon began delivering pans of hot food to our shelter! Pans of large pork chops and fried chicken, mashed potatoes, rolls, green beans, and desert! We could hardly believe how God was providing! Yet, He came through time-after-time when we called!

Well the storm bore down on us during that three week period and God stood between us and them and protected His people there at Otter Creek, just like He did thousands of years ago during Moses' time.

Flood Waters

Living in the church house with 75 other people can be quite interesting at times! The flood waters invaded Otter Creek sometime during the three week deluge when the ditches that drain the highway system and the planted pine forests finally filled up.

The area is quite dry normally due to Georgia Pacific and other timber companies establishing an elaborate system of drainage ditches that empty water pretty fast out of the areas they have planted pines in, which is most of north central Florida.

The days of virgin forests are over forever in our fair state due to the lust for wood products made from the fast growing pines that are usually harvested every 14-15 years. Most of the hardwood hammocks have been cleared and drained to accommodate more rows of unsightly planted pine!

We were high and dry at the church when the flood waters came. Many of the roads were impassible for a while due to the high water. Highway US 19 stayed dry although Highway SR 24 between Otter Creek and Bronson was shut down for a while due to the Wacasassa River flooding.

Most of the lime rock graded roads into Gulf Hammock were underwater as well. We had church members that lived down some of these roads and could not get back to their homes due to the high water.

A few of them made it to the safety of the church with us but there were others that were stranded. Rescue operations were started and the Harmony Baptist Disaster Team responded along with FEMA and others who began trying to locate and evacuate the residents that were in the outlying wooded areas of Gulf Hammock.

One particular family we had not heard from for almost a week was the Holmes family, who lived deep in the woods at the old McMillan Place. We had tried to call them but the phone lines were all down in that part of the woods and never did reach them.

We assumed that they had gone to Tampa to be with their parents to escape the hurricanes and the flooding they brought. I asked the Harmony Disaster Team if they would try and make it to the McMillan place to check on the Holmes family to make sure they weren't stranded there.

Frankie Asbell and Rock Meeks were two men that volunteered to make the long trek there and back.

It was around 6 miles back into the woods were the Holmes lived. They took an aluminum "john" boat and started down the flooded grade back to where they lived. The last mile or more of the journey the road was under water for the most part. As they approached the road back into the McMillan place they stopped to listen for sounds that might indicate that there was life there.

To their amazement they could hear a small generator running. They yelled a few times to see if anyone could hear them. Sure enough, shouts came back to them!

They soon found the whole family safe and sound back on their property. The 40 acre McMillan Place had been built years earlier on the highest place they could find.

This was their salvation and it kept their double-wide and other hunting camps and trailers above the flooding. However, it didn't keep them from being stranded there for four or five days without power or phone service! Large trees were down across the road going into their place and there was only one way in, and that was by small boat. They were overjoyed to see the rescue guys showing up to help them.

There were 8 people stranded in there if my count is still accurate. The grandmother, mother, and two small children were the first to load up for the trip out.

The others had been cutting trees that blocked their road and decided to finish doing that before they tried to get out. They had a 4x4 truck with large tires that they felt could make the trip out once the trees were cleared.

The first to load up in the small boat for the trip to safety was the grandmother and mother along with the two little children.

The grandmother and mother shed tears of joy knowing that they had been rescued and would now be safe at the church! Within a day the rest of the family made it to our little church shelter in Otter Creek.

Frankie and Rock

Without Frankie and Rock making that long trip to help bring them out, they would have been stranded another two or three days. They were hungry, wet, and tired, yet safe! They stayed with us at the shelter for the remainder of the two weeks or so that we were there.

That story is so much like God's rescue mission for lost humanity! We humans are stranded by the flood waters of our sins with no hope of escaping unless someone intervenes.

Many think they don't need help and try to survive life and eternity on their own. Yet in the end they find like we all do that we are stranded without Him! Yet the search goes on throughout history! God is continually seeking the lost to pull them to safety. Our job is to be part of God's rescue team. God's Word says, *"For the Son of man is come to seek and to save that which was lost."* (Luke 19:10)

The rescue mission that day, and others like it during the "Hurricanes from Hell", reminded me of the parable of the lost sheep that Jesus told:

"If a man has a hundred sheep and one of them gets lost, what will he do? Won't he leave the ninety-nine others in the wilderness and go to search for the one that is lost until he finds it? And when he has found it, he will joyfully carry it home on his shoulders. When he arrives, he will call together his friends and neighbors, saying, 'Rejoice with me because I have found my lost sheep'."

Joy in Heaven

In the same way, there is more joy in heaven over one lost sinner who repents and returns to God than over ninety-nine others who are righteous and haven't strayed away!" (Luke 15:4-7) (NLT)

If you are lost out there in the storms of life; know this for sure, The Savior is on a rescue mission and is looking for you! Hold on a little bit longer and listen for His call. He'll be there soon!

Lives Were Touched

We opened up the shelter at Otter Creek during that time to help minister to those that were in need due to the storm. There were many who were safe and warm in their own homes, hunkered down to ride out the storm, but I am so glad that we listened to God and opened up the church shelter.

My life was forever touched by being a part of something that was far bigger than we could have ever imagined! The hard-working, dedicated members and friends of Otter Creek Baptist Church that cooked, cleaned, rescued, and repaired storm damage, went down in God's history book that year as being one of the groups in our state that didn't run and hide from trouble!

We met the "Hurricane from Hell" face-to-face and ministered to those that needed us right then. I thank God for that opportunity!

Harmony Baptist Disaster Team

Another special group of men and women who also volunteered under the direction of Dr. Jerry Nash, Director of Missions for Harmony Baptist Association, are the members of the Harmony Disaster Relief Team.

These special people are always on standby for emergencies such as the "Hurricanes from Hell." They worked tirelessly during and after the storms to help in the cleanup and recovery of those whose homes were affected the most. Without them the job would have been impossible!

The Disaster Relief Teams of the Southern Baptist Convention are always on ready status to respond to any and all natural disasters across our nation.

The Harmony Team dovetails with the other SBC Teams in place across our nation. During the "Hurricane from Hell" we not only had the local Harmony Baptist Team working our area, we also had a team from Texas working alongside us as well.

As I was thinking about the storms that year and how close they came to us, I was reminded of the Scripture that says:

(Isaiah 43:2)*"When thou passest through the waters, I will be with thee; and through the rivers, they shall not overflow thee: when thou walkest through the fire, thou shalt not be burned; neither shall the flame kindle upon thee."*

Just as God delivered Israel of old, He still remembers His promise to His people today! He kept us and protected us from the "Hurricane from Hell!" He is a great God and worthy of our service and praise!

God Spared Our Home

Oh, by the way, remember our home that we boarded up and left when the storm was approaching? We left it not knowing if it would be standing when we returned.

God took good care of it just as we had asked Him to! We still live there today! Our little sign at the front door reads: *"Bless this house or Lord we pray, keep it safe by night and day."* I learned once again, when you obey God, and do whatever He is telling you to do, He has your back!

Mighty Whitey

I never thought that "Mighty Whitey" would be of much use other than for hunting season. My old 1985 Chevrolet Diesel 4 x 4 Military Blazer had been dubbed "Mighty Whitey" early on when I first traded another truck for it. It had very tall, non-directional mud grips on it that made it sit pretty high off the ground. It was painted white, from which it derived its name.

The "mighty" part came from the fact that it could pull! You could hardly find a mud-hole or muddy place that "Mighty Whitey" could not pull out of!

My grandkids still love the old truck all though it is parked in "semi-retirement" right now, awaiting some tender love and care.

The role that this strong little truck played in the "Hurricane from Hell" came about during and after the storm. During the storm it was the perfect truck for making it to and from washed out flooded roads and to pick up people or retrieve items from homes that were flooded.

The main role it played was a guide truck during the recovery period when FEMA finally came to survey the damage to the area and give assistance to those in the outlying areas.

They didn't know their way around the woods and where the people were, but I did. When they needed someone to guide them I volunteered. I drove my old faithful "Mighty Whitey" and they followed in their newer 4 x 4 fancy trucks.

The devastation in our area was mostly downed trees that covered many roads, roofs that were blown off or crushed by falling limbs, or massive flooding. We rode for miles throughout the Gulf Hammock area as I led them to all the known roads and settlements where people lived.

The water was much deeper than I could have imagined. We were performing these missions after the waters had subsided for a few days so we missed the peak of the flood waters which was a good thing!

The water was so deep on the roads in many places that I could reach out the driver's window and touch the water with my fingertips. The old Detroit diesel motor and the tough 4 x 4 running gear in that truck was the perfect match for what I put that truck through!

I originally traded for it so that I could use it in hunting season when we were still hunting deer with hounds. It was the perfect ride for that, enabling you to go anywhere you needed when the deer took to the swampy areas! Dog hunting began to fade in Florida and many of us eventually got rid of our hound dogs. The need for a strong 4 x 4 was not as great in the areas that I hunted in after that, yet I kept the old truck anyway. It will be passed on to my grandchildren one day when the time is right.

During the "Hurricane from Hell" the old truck earned it's keep by being the right vehicle for that time. I was so glad that it was available to search and assist those that had storm damage to their homes and property. Little did I dream that old "Mighty Whitey" would be called upon to perform such important work! I felt honored that God was able to use it as He had our little church in the middle of nowhere called Otter Creek!

God works like that so many times. He chooses obscure people and odd things to get the job done. Have you ever used a shoe or some other object other than a hammer to drive a nail into a wall? Most people have. When asked why they used a shoe, they will invariably say, *"Because I didn't have a hammer!"*

Many times you just use whatever you can find to get the job done! That's how God has worked throughout history. He uses whoever is available! He did that whenever He wanted to get something done.

God Always Provides

The Bible records a true story of Jesus doing just that. Jesus soon saw a huge crowd of people coming to look for him. Turning to Philip, he asked, *"Where can we buy bread to feed all these people?"* He was testing Philip, for he already knew what he was going to do. Philip replied, *"Even if we worked for months, we wouldn't have enough money to feed them!"*

Then Andrew, Simon Peter's brother, spoke up. "There's a young boy here with five barley loaves and two fish. But what good is that with this huge crowd?" *"Tell everyone to sit down,"* Jesus said. So they all sat down on the grassy slopes. (The men alone numbered about 5,000.)

Then Jesus took the loaves, gave thanks to God, and distributed them to the people. Afterward he did the same with the fish. And they all ate as much as they wanted. (John 6:5-11) (NLT)

We were used of God to meet many needs during the "Hurricane from Hell," not because we were super Christians or the best God could find. We were used of God during that time because we were available to God, just like the little boy that gave Jesus his bread and fish.

We were just the instrument that was nearby when God wanted to do a great work! Mighty Whitey played a role because I made it available to God during and after that time. God is continually working all around us. If we become aware of what His objectives are and what His work looks like, we will realize that He has called us to be His helpers.

Chapter 35

Salt Island and Salt Kettle Remains

Picture courtesy of Google Earth

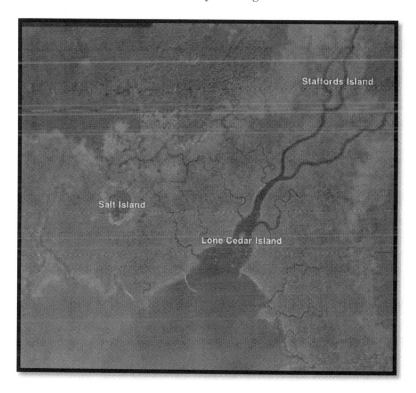

Anybody who has ever lived around Otter Creek, Gulf Hammock, or Cedar Key knows about Salt Island.

As you can see from the picture from Google Earth, when you are coming out of the Wacasassa River, you can look toward Cedar Key and the elevated tree line of Salt Island stands out above the coastal marsh. An enlarged view shows the trees with the large pond.

When we moved to Otter Creek in 1954 we hunted around Camp E and the old Watson Place. I also wandered all over the marsh and shot ducks on the ponds that are scattered throughout that area.

Picture courtesy of Google Earth

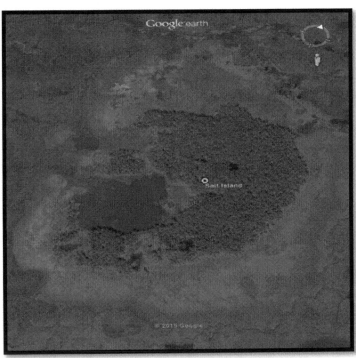

Salt Island is located in the Wacasassa Bay State Preserve, which is a coastal marsh area extending from Cedar Key, Florida to the Withlacoochee River. This preserve is bounded by land owned by the Georgia Pacific Paper Company. These two large tracts are collectively known as Gulf Hammock.

Large Pond

This is a close up view of the large pond seen in the picture from Google Earth. This is a salt water pond and it is filled with redfish and trout. This land belongs to the State of Florida now, but back in 1954, when we moved to Otter Creek, this was still open to hunting.

Years ago, Grady Phelps Jr. and some of his friends had the bright idea of seining this pond. They loaded their long net on a truck and began the difficult drive in.

Long before they ever reached Salt Island they had to give up on the idea because their net had been destroyed by the branches and limbs along the trail that made it all but impossible for a vehicle to get through, much less a truck loaded down with a long net.

Although I never saw them myself, most of the folks around Otter Creek knew there were remains of broken salt pots on Salt Island. It was common knowledge that the remains were what was left of some large iron pots once used to boil water and make salt.

The Value of Salt

Research reveals that during the Civil War the price of salt was unbelievable. Before refrigeration, salt was the primary means of preserving meat and fish for future consumption. It took two bushels (about 110 pounds) to cure 1,000 pounds of pork. It took 1.25 bushels to cure 500 pounds of beef. Salt was also used to tan leather, fix the dyes in military uniforms, and feed livestock. In some cases, salt was even used for legal tender.

Dr. Judy Bense

According to Dr. Judy Bense, with Unearthing Florida: "The Union strategy of cutting off supplies from the north and blockading southern ports deeply impacted the Confederate governments' ability to import salt. By 1863, production was left to the coastal State of Florida. With government incentives, salt work operations sprang up quickly along the state's coastline. In response, the Union navy was given the task of shutting these salt works down. But, the job proved impossible, because as soon one such operation was destroyed, it simply relocated to a different spot along the vast coast and resumed production."

Toni Collins

According to Toni Collins, Levy County Historian, "In pre-Civil War Florida, the price of salt was 65 cents per bushel. By the end of 1861, the price had risen to $3.00 locally and $20 per bushel in the rest of the Confederacy. Toward the end of the war prices reached as high as $50 per bushel."

The Raid on Cedar Key

On October 4, 1862, Federal forces raided the salt works in Cedar Key. According to Toni Collins, "The U.S. gunboat Somerset attacked the salt works in Cedar Key which was located in the vicinity of **present Live Oak Key.**"

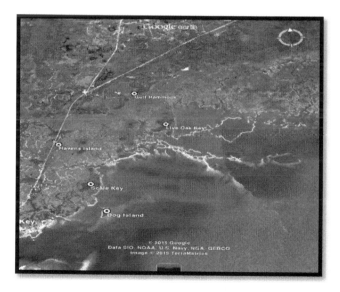

On October 6, with the assistance of the gunboat Tahoma, the union forces destroyed 50-60 large boilers, capable of producing 150 pounds of salt every 24 hours."

The pot in the following picture is like the ones destroyed in the raid in 1861. This pot can still be seen at the Cedar Key Museum.

Mystery Solved

We mentioned previously that everybody around Otter Creek back in the 1950s knew about the salt pots on Salt Island. We also knew of the 1861 "Yankee" raid on the Salt Works in Cedar Key.

Up until this month (February 2015) many of us assumed that in that raid, the Yankee ships had sailed into Wacasassa Bay and had destroyed the salt works on Salt Island. **This was not accurate.**

My Question on FaceBook

We had posted the following question on Facebook last week (February 3, 2015).

"I need some help from somebody who has a knowledge of the history of Levy County.

I'm trying to finish my book on Otter Creek and Levy County and I need some accurate information on Salt Island and Salt Key.

There was a large site in Levy County where the South made salt. They had huge kettles in which they boiled salt water. The Union troops came in and destroyed the salt production.

When I came to Otter Creek in 1954, I was told by the locals that the remains of those salt pots were still present on Salt Island.

Our Question Was

Is there a difference between Salt Key and Salt Island?

Did the Union troops destroy the pots on Salt Island?

How about emailing me any information you may have on this subject.gk122532@gmail.com

Yeartys to the Rescue

Sammy and Evelyn Yearty provided us with some interesting information on this in a Prospective by M.F.

Dickinson and G.W. Edwardson, titled, *"The Salt Works of Salt Island, Florida."*

According to our research, Archeologist Martin Dickinson made some excavations on Salt Island back in 1977 and he made some interesting discoveries.

Their project located the remains of two furnaces and five iron kettles.

OUR CONCLUSION

1. We have concluded this week through our research that the salt works that were destroyed in Cedar Key and the salt remains on Salt Island were two entirely different sites.

The salt works in Cedar Key was located near Live Oak Key and Station Number Four.

The salt works on Salt Island was located near the Wacasassa River.

2. The salt works in Cedar Key was *much larger* than the salt works on Salt Island.

The salt works in Cedar Key produced 150 pounds of salt every 24 hours.

The Union forces destroyed 50-60 large pots like the one seen in the following picture.

3. The salt works in Cedar Key was large enough to be *viewed as a threat* to the Union forces. The salt works on Salt Island was *not viewed as a threat.*

According to Archeologist Martin Dickenson, "The salt works on Salt Island do seem to fit the picture of a small clandestine operation."

Dickenson also said: "The salt works on Salt Island were of such a small scale that their operation would seem to be associated with either plantation or a group of local farmers."

There were two salt works. One in Cedar Key and the other on Salt Island. Both locations have remains of iron kettles used to make salt.

The Union forces destroyed the salt works in Cedar Key, but contrary to what we had been led to believe, they did not destroy the salt works located on Salt Island near the Wacasassa River. The salt works in Cedar Key was in operation during the Civil War. The salt works located on Salt Island was probably in operation after the Civil War.

Note: We could be wrong and we welcome your comments. You may contact us at: gk122532@gmail.com

4. Another interesting fact discovered by Dickenson was the salt content of the large pond on Salt Island was higher than the creeks and tidal ponds in that area.

Chapter 36

The Rest of the Story - 50 Years Later

This is our daughter Sandy Keith Robertson, who was born in Otter Creek, fishing out in the Wacasassa Bay where she fished as a child. It is interesting that Sandy's daughter, Angela Robertson Watson, married Kyle Watson, the grandson of Dewitt Watson Jr., who first introduced this author to the Wacasassa flats.

Sandy is fishing the same flats she fished on as a child.

Sandy and her grandchildren are fishing the same area 50 years later.

This picture is of Sandy, Robbie (her husband) and their son, Daniel, his wife Lacy, and their family, fishing the same area.

This is our grandson, Kyle Watson and his son, fishing the same waters Kyle's grandfather, Dewitt Watson introduced us to when we first moved to Otter Creek back in 1954.

This is Sandy's daughter, Christie, with her little two year old niece, holding up her first scallop out of Cedar key.

Grandma Tuelah (Ya Ya) Cleaning Scallops

Yours truly with a nice Cedar Key Grouper

Pastor Bill Keith with a nice pair of Levy County hogs

Wild Hogs

Our grandson, Daniel Robertson, Sandy's second son, must smell like a wild animal. No matter where you put him on a stand, the deer and wild animals are attracted to him. Look at the next picture and you will understand what I mean.

Daniel Robertson feeding "wild" Hogs

The Booger Stand

One day, while hunting in "The Preacher Club" down near Inglis, our dogs jumped, what we thought was a deer. Everything was going normal until we heard our son, Stevie, shoot.

Immediately after Stevie shot, he got on his walkie-talkie, and with a shaky voice said, "I've just killed something and I have no idea what it is. The dogs ran it to me, but when I killed it, and the dogs reached it, they smelled it and backed away."

We all hurried up there to see what was going on and when we reached Stevie, the dogs, and the "thing," none of us knew what that "thing" was. It was fresh but it stunk to high heaven. What is this strange Thing?

After asking around, we later assumed that this "thing" was an exotic animal that had somehow escaped from a private preserve located near our lease. From that time on, we called that place where Stevie shot the "thing" the Booger Stand. Perhaps some of our readers can help us identify this strange, foul-smelling, creature.

Note: Why waste time going all the way to Africa to hunt? Life in Levy County is always exciting.

We are Still Enjoying Our Hunting Camp

Chapter 37

People Who Touched Our Lives

My Dear Friend Dick Parnell

From left to right: Zelda, Dick, Kaye, and Francis

Dick went to be with the Lord on April 25, 2015. He was one of the dearest friends I ever had. RIP my brother.

Randall "Dick" Parnell, 76, of Chiefland, went to be with the Lord on Saturday, April 25, 2015, at North Florida Regional Hospital in Gainesville.

He was born June 29, 1938 in Gulf Hammock to Claude and Donna Parnell.

Dick graduated from Bronson High School and proudly served his country in the U.S. Army for three years and was part of the 101st Airborne Division. He was a loving, Christian husband, father, grandfather and brother.

He was preceded in death by his parents and his brother, Wayne Parnell. Dick was a long time member of First Baptist Church of Chiefland and enjoyed his Sunday School Class and all of the church activities.

He was a member of the Magee Branch Hunting Club. Dick worked for many years at the Florida Highway Patrol before becoming a partner in the Beauchamp Hardware Store for many years before his retirement. He found enjoyment in hunting, fishing, supporting the Chiefland High School, but the most enjoyment in life was his love for his family.

Mr. Parnell is survived by his wife of 50 years, Frances Beauchamp Parnell; his son, Kyle (Shari) Parnell; his daughter, Kimberly (Avery) Baker, all of Chiefland; two sisters, Kay (John) Rogers and Zelda (Johnny) Lott of Bronson; grandsons, Parrish, Payton and Payne Parnell, Kaiden and Karsen Baker; a granddaughter, Adysen Baker, and many, many other loving family and friends.

Expressions of sympathy may also be made to the Building Fund of First Baptist Church of Chiefland.

Visitation will be Monday, April 27 from 5-7 p.m. at the chapel of Langford-Rogers Memorial Funeral Home. Funeral Services will be Tuesday, April 28 at 3 p.m. at the First Baptist Church of Chiefland. A committal service will follow at the Chiefland Cemetery.

Langford-Rogers Memorial Funeral Home- 1301 North Young Blvd. Chiefland, FL., (352) 493-0050 is honored to serve the Parnell Family.

Mr. Nick and Mrs. Anna West

We mentioned in chapter one how that Mrs. Anna and I got off to a bad start. However, I want to go on record and say that Mr. Nick and Mrs. Anna West were faithful members of the Otter Creek Church and they were always good to us.

Mr. Nick even helped me pay my tuition one year while I was commuting to the University of Florida.

And one year, when I was invited to speak at Baccalaureate in Bronson, Mrs. Anna bought me a brand new suit to preach in.

I will always be grateful for the West family.

Mr. Bert and Mrs. Ruby West

Mr. Bert and Nick West were brothers and operated a large turpentine business in Levy County at one time. By the time we arrived they had sold their business and had leased hundreds of acres of land to the timber companies.

One thing we need to mention about the West brothers, is that during the Rosewood massacre, the West brothers hid a large number of Black families in their barns where they fed them and protected them.

Lewis and Margaret Renfroe

Lewis and Margaret Renfroe were our next door neighbors in Otter Creek. We both lived directly across the road from the Otter Creek School.

Mrs. Margaret, the daughter of Nick and Anna West, taught school in Otter Creek and Mr. Louis had a logging business. He also served as the Treasurer of the Otter Creek Baptist Church.

Another important contribution of Mr. Lewis is that he and Sam Standridge were the only people in town who had four wheel drive jeeps. We cannot count the times we got stuck and had to walk to Otter Creek to get Mr. Lewis to pull us out.

Mrs. Margaret was the faithful pianist for the Otter Creek Baptist Church, and as far as I can remember, she never missed one service for the entire five years I served as pastor there.

Jonel Holmes

I Wonder if we could have survived in those days without the help of Jonel Holmes. Jonel was the daughter of Buford and Liza Holmes and the sister of Donald, Melba, Hilda, and Glenn.

Jonel was always willing and ready to help us in any way she could. She was especially good at baby-sitting. She had a way with kids and all of the kids in Otter Creek loved her.

On one particular occasion in 1959, Jonel "saved the day." I'm almost embarrassed to even tell this story, but I will.

Like the immature young man I was, I had gone to New Orleans as a chaperone for the Senior Class of Bronson High School.

Tuelah was not only pregnant, but to make matters worse, I took our only vehicle we had and left my pregnant wife at home without transportation. Jonel volunteered to come stay with Tuelah and the four kids while I was gone.

In the middle of the night that week, Tuelah began having labor pains. I might add that, according to calculations, the baby was not due yet. However, the labor pains began and I was somewhere between Otter Creek and New Orleans and Jonel was the only one who could help, and she did!

Jonel quickly got out of bed, dressed, went next door, got our neighbors, Lewis and Margaret Renfore, out of bed and told them of the emergency.

They got out of bed, dressed, and drove Tuelah to the hospital in Gainesville to have our fifth child while Jonel stayed with our other four children.

Jonel was always there when we needed her.

"Thank you Dear Jonel."

Mrs. Red and Mr. "Fido" Williams

Mrs. Red and "Fido" were great friends. They lived right behind Mr. Nick and Mrs. Anna. Mrs. Red baby sat for us a lot and in return for all she did for us, we drove their daughter, Linda, who had polio, to the doctor in Jacksonville. In fact, the only time Tuelah and I had any time off together was when Mrs. Red kept our five kids.

Our children all remember staying with Mrs. Red. She didn't have any toys like kids today, but she had a yard full of chickens and our kids would amuse themselves for hours playing with chickens in the dirt.

Fido told me once that, years ago when he lived in Inglis, that he could have traded a 55 gallon drum of moonshine for several acres of waterfront property on the Withlacoochee River. He said "he kicked himself" over and over for not making the trade.

Pastor Was Chauffeur

Back in those days, we pastors served as the chauffeurs for anybody in town who needed a ride to the doctor. I can't count the times we drove Mrs. Red's daughter, Emily to the children's clinic in Jacksonville. Their poor little girl had been afflicted with polio.

The Last Ride

On another occasion, I was getting ready to take two pregnant women from Otter Creek to Gainesville for their doctor's appointments.

Just about the time I was pulling out from our home, my friend, Charlie Richelieu from St. Petersburg, pulled up in a brand new Plymouth Fury. You will remember that they were really "hot" and I was dying to try it out.

I jumped in the driver's seat; Charlie hopped in the passenger's seat; the two pregnant women got in the back seat and we were off.

When we crossed the Wacasassa Bridge on SR 24, we were doing over 100 mph.

Those two pregnant ladies didn't utter a word for the rest of the trip to Gainesville.

And for some strange reason, neither of them ever asked me for a ride again!

Mrs. Ruth Revels - The Dog woman

Everybody knew Mrs. Ruth. We called her "The Dog Woman." She loved dogs and hunting and boarded dogs in her kennel in Otter Creek. Mrs. Ruth even kept our two Beagles, "Shorty" and "Little Red," when we moved down to Cape Canaveral in 1968-1969.

Mrs. Ruth Revels - We called her The "Dog Woman"
She loved dogs

Mrs. Ruth and Dick Parnell

She had no patience with people who were mean to animals. I remember one time, Dick Parnell and I got stuck coming in from Camp E.

He had a pile of dogs in the back of his truck. Mrs. Ruth happened to come by and offered to pull him out with her tow chain. About the time she got the chain hooked up, Dick's dogs started fighting and he grabbed a limb and begin to beat the dog that was fighting.

Mrs. Ruth stopped, looked Dick square in the eye and said, "You touch that dog one more time and I will leave you right here."

Dick threw the stick down and thank goodness, Mrs. Ruth pulled us out.

Dog Funeral Home

One time Mrs. Ruth was boarding a dog for someone and their dog got sick and died. When the owners came to pick up their dead dog, Mrs. Ruth had the dog laying up in bed, covered up, with its tiny head on a pillow. It was like a dog funeral home. She really cared for animals.

Madge Casey: Postmistress

Madge was the Postmaster in Gulf Hammock when we moved to Otter Creek back in 1954. The post office was located in the old commissary and Madge seemed to know everybody in Levy County.

No one ever received one of those "return to sender" notices, because in Gulf Hammock, the mail ALWAYS arrived at its destination.

One example of that was when my younger brother, Louis Keith, served as game warden in that area. Jody McCreary, a close friend (now a relative) in Tarpon Springs sent my brother Louis, a letter. Now this was no ordinary letter. Jody wrote this letter on a piece of brown paper sack. He addressed this strange letter like this:

> Louis Keith
> Out by Mr. Bird
> Gulf Hammock

Can you believe that Louis received that letter? He received the letter because Madge knew exactly where Louis lived "out by Mr. Bird." That's just the way things were back in the *good ole days*.

Toad Curry

Two things come to mind when I think of Toad. The first story I recall is that Toad was one of the first kids in Otter Creek to have a pair of lace up dress shoes. His parents were so proud.

But what they didn't know, was that Toad would leave home for school with his lace up shoes on, but before he arrived at school, he would take the shoes off and hide them in the bushes. He was afraid the other kids would laugh at him because nearly all of the kids in Otter Creek went barefooted.

The other memory I have of Toad was that he had, what was probably the fastest car in Levy County. You will remember that up until 1955, all Chevrolets had in-line six cylinder engines. In 1955 they came out with a V-8 and it was really "hot." The 1956 and 1957 models were even hotter with 4 barrel carbs and stick shifts.

In 1957, Toad bought a brand new Chevrolet and this one had something nobody around Otter Creek had ever seen. It didn't have carbs. It had a fuel injection system. Nobody knew how it worked, but it did, and it would literally outrun everything else on the highway.

It would hide the speedometer, which registered 120 mph.

There was only one problem. Sometimes Toad would turn the key off and shut it down at a filling station and when he was ready to leave, the car just wouldn't start.

This happened one day at Howard Williams' filling station, which was located where the present Otter Creek Post Office is today. They tried everything they knew to do and it still refused to start.

When something like this happens around Otter Creek, you don't call 911. You call Willie Berryhill. If Willie couldn't fix it, it couldn't be fixed.

On this particular day, Willie had a garage just north of the intersection of US 19 and SR 24. So, they called Willie to come down to the station and get Toad's Chevrolet going again.

Willie walked up with confidence and raised the hood. He looked at that strange motor, backed up and began to shake his head. He had never seen anything like that before. As far as I can remember, this was the first time in Levy County history that Willie couldn't get a car going.

That's what I remember about Toad.

Monroe (Suwannee) Kilcrease

We called Monroe Kilcrease "Suwannee" because he operated the Suwannee store on Main Street in Otter creek.

For some reason, what we call Main Street is actually Third Street. Anyway, the Suwannee store was across the street from the Smith's Store. The Masonic Lodge met upstairs and Murrell Watson and his family lived right behind it. On the West side of the store was the dirt road that led south to the checking station and Williams' Fish Camp.

"Suwannee" was a faithful member of the Otter Creek Baptist Church and was good to us. He allowed us to get groceries on credit and pay for them on time. Bologna was the cheapest meat you could buy back then. We often joke and say, *"If you put all of the bologna our kids ate in one wad it would reach from Flat Branch to the six-mile still."*

Suwannee and his family were also good friends. His grandchildren, Mike and Iris Meeks, were two of our son Bill's, best friends.

Their mother, Ottie was Suwannee's daughter. She was married to "Cub" Meeks, the brother of Liza Holmes and Coot Meeks.

Mike and Iris' older sister Carolyn is married to "Uncle Jimmy" (Little Coot) Meeks, whose parents are the late Rufas (Coot) and Marie Meeks.

Suwannee Saved the Day

One day I had taken a group of teenagers from the church to Fanning Springs. I was sitting up on the high dive, enjoying the sunshine and watching the kids, when I happened to look back and saw Grandma Standridge (Sam and James' mother) pull into the sandy parking lot in her green and white 1956 Chevrolet.

She began walking toward us nervously and waving her arms. When she got close enough for us to hear her she shouted: "There's a bunch of cars parked around the church and there's a bunch of preachers there."

I had no idea what was going on but decided it was time to leave the spring and head to Otter Creek. What I had forgotten was that once a month there was a pastor's conference. The churches in the Harmony Baptist Association would take turns hosting the meeting and the church would provide the meals. So there we were. I was at Fanning Springs with the church kids. Tuelah was home taking care of our kids and there were approximately thirty pastors at the church expecting a nice meal. Here is how Suwannee Kilcrease saved the day. He quickly gathered up some groceries, closed the store, and went over to the pastorium, gave Tuelah the food, and if I remember correctly, I think he even stayed there and helped her cook. I walked in just in time to ask the blessing. It was a miracle that I wasn't fired or divorced.

"Bug" Watkins

Another "famous" Gulf Hammock resident was "Bug Watkins." Bug and I were friends for years. I first met him when I became the pastor in Otter Creek and visited in every home in Otter Creek and Gulf Hammock.

I remember the day I met Bug and his wife. They invited Tuelah and me into their home and we had a great visit. As we were leaving, we were standing on his front porch. I happened to look up and right above our heads was a nice double barrel shotgun stuck between the rafters and the tin roof, pointing to the front yard.

His daughter Eugenia and her husband Willard McElveen also hunted with our family back in the *good ole days*.

Speaking of hunting, "Bug" was probably the most famous hunter in Levy County. It would take a book to record all of the stories told about old "Bug." One night he got caught fire hunting. He and the game warden got into a tussle and Bug ended up getting shot in the foot.

How Bug got His Name

One of the most interesting stories I remember about Bug was how he got his name. Probably very few people know this.

Dick Parnell told me that when Bug started to school the teacher was getting the names of all of his students. When he came to Bug, the teacher asked him his full name. Bug told him it was "Bug" Watkins.

The teacher asked him again about his real first name. Again Bug answered that it was "Bug" and that was the only name he had ever had. The teacher's name was "Tom Price."

The school teacher recorded his name as "Tom Price Watkins" and that was how Bug Watkins got his name.

Chapter 38

Honorable Mention

Many of the people who were my age or teenagers when I came to Otter Creek, have gone on to become prominent leaders in their respective communities. We want to mention a few of them.

Gary Lott

The late Gary Lott graduated from Bronson High School in 1959 and later became the President of Flagler College in Palatka, Florida.

Luther Drummond

I remember two things about Luther Drummond. He was a close friend of Elwin Standridge and Luther's grandfather had a hunting camp across the road from our camp down near the old Williams' Fish Camp. Luther has done real well. He owns Drummond Community Bank which has offices in: Archer, Bronson, Cross City, Chiefland, Cedar Key, Inglis, Mayo, Trenton, Old Town & Williston. Luther reminds us: *"There's One Near You!"*

Grady Phelps

Grady Phelps Jr. (Otter Creek), retired as a Colonel in the Florida Game Commission. Grady was the second highest ranking officer in the commission.

Dale Phelps

Dale was the second oldest son in the Phelps family. He, like two of his brothers, served as a game warden before entering a career in publishing.

Gary Phelps

Grady's younger brother Gary (Otter creek), retired as a Major in the Florida Game Commission.

Donald Holmes

Donald Holmes (Otter Creek) served several terms as a County Commissioner.

Doyle and Ann (Renfroe) McCall

Doyle and Ann came from Gulf Hammock and Otter Creek respectively. Ann followed her mother into teaching and was a very popular teacher in the Levy County Schools. Doyle McCall spent his entire 39-year professional career at Chiefland High School. During his years there, he served as history teacher, coach, Athletic Director, Dean of Students, Assistant Principal and Principal. In 1988 he was inducted into the Florida Athletic Coaches Association Hall of Fame.

Sammy Yearty

Sammy Yearty (Gulf Hammock) also served several terms as a County Commissioner.

Mac McCoy

Mac McCoy (Bronson) served several terms as the Clerk of the Levy County Court.

W. O. and Luther Beauchamp

Brothers Luther and W. O. Beauchamp Jr. (Chiefland) both became successful attorneys. W. O. also served as our Levy County Judge. His son, Brett now serves as second in command in the Levy County Sheriff's office.

Elwin Standridge

Elwin and his wife, Doris (Kirkland) Standridge owned and operated a very successful pine straw business.

Stevie Bird

Stevie Bird (Gulf Hammock) became a successful businessman with his own insurance company in Ocala, Florida.

Murray Tillis

Murray Tillis (Chiefland), the son of Melba (Holmes) Tillis and the grandson of Buford Holmes, has become one of the most successful farmers in Levy County.

Jack Foley

Dr. Jack Foley (Gulf Hammock) earned his PhD and taught math at the University of Florida.

Don Foley

Don Foley (Gulf Hammock) also served several terms as a County Commissioner.

Danny Shipp

I first met Danny Shipp when he was a kid, working at the Pat & Mac filling station in Gulf Hammock. Danny was so short when he worked at the filling station he had to stand on a box to reach the cash register. Danny is now serving as the Clerk of the Court in Levy County.

Linda Fugate

Linda Fugate, the daughter of Dorothy (Berryhill) Daniels (Gulf Hammock) now serves as the Tax Collector for Levy County.

Aline Smith

Aline Smith, one of the "Smith Girls" Bill wrote about from Gulf Hammock, now has a restaurant in Trenton where she won the "2014 Business of the Year Award." Her restaurant is named "The Cracker Box."

Rock Meeks

Rock Meeks (Ellzey) was elected to serve as a Levy County Commissioner and was sworn in on November 18, 2014.

Nancy Scarborough

Nancy Scarborough, the daughter of Betty Jo, and the granddaughter of Sam and Dottie Standridge (Otter Creek) has served as the Coach's Secretary for the University of Florida Gators since the days of Coach Steve Spurrier.

Notice

Dear Reader:

There is no doubt in my mind that I have overlooked someone important. Believe me. This was not intentional.

As you read this book and you know of someone or something I have (unintentionally) failed to mention, *please let me know* so that I can update this book before printing the second edition.

Sincerely,

Gene Keith

gk122532@gmail.com

Chapter 39

Country Cooking Recipes

Tuelah and I were coming through Trenton the other day (March 10, 2015) and a thought came to me. I was about to publish this book and remembered that I had forgotten to include some *good ole* country recipes.

Aline Smith, one of the "Smith girls" from Gulf Hammock has a little restaurant in Trenton appropriately called "The Cracker Box."

We pulled in hoping that Aline would be there and she was. I asked her if she happened to have some good old country recipes I could include in this book.

She agreed and here are a few of them.

Fried Cat Squirrel

Ingredients

Six young and tender squirrels
2 cups of flour
4 cups of oil
Salt and pepper

Directions

Clean the squirrels and cut them into pieces
Salt, pepper, and flour the pieces
Get your grease hot.
Put in grease and fry until they're done.

Swamp Cabbage

Ingredients

Two hearts of cabbage out of the cabbage tree.
One pack of hawg jowls.
Add 1/8 of a cup of sugar.

Directions

Cook hawg jowls in pot until grease cooks out.
Add about 6 cups of water.
Salt, lots of pepper and the sugar.
Add the heart of the cabbage tree and cook for about an hour or until the cabbage is soft.

Blue Crabs and Gravy

Ingredients

1 loaf of white bread
1 dozen crabs cleaned
1 chopped onion
1 cup of oil
1 cup of flour
Salt and Pepper

Directions

Let Oil get hot and add flour.
Stir Until dark brown almost burning.
Add about 1 ½ gallons of water it will be thin but that's okay. Add the onions let boil until onions are done.
Add Crabs cook until crabs are red about 10 -15 minutes.
Ball bread up and dip into crab gravy.
Salt to taste and add lots of black pepper!

(It'll make you want to slap your momma!!)

About the Author

Gene Keith was born William Eugene Keith in Tarpon Springs, Florida, on December 25, 1932. His parents were Walter Keith Jr. and Louise (Campbell) Keith.

He graduated from the Tarpon Springs High School in 1950, married his sweetheart, Tuelah Evelyn Riviere in 1952.

Gene became a Christian in 1952 and entered the ministry in 1953.

The following information is from an article titled, **"Circling the Wagons,"** which appeared in the Florida Baptist Witness January 28, 2013 Joni B. Hannigan, Managing Editor.

"Gene Keith is part of a ten generation legacy of pioneer Christian leaders from Kentucky, Texas, and Florida. Since 1773 when John Keith hosted the first meeting of Virginia's Ten Mile Baptist Church, the Keith men for at least ten generations have led their congregations as Baptist preachers, elders or deacons, to be pioneers in sharing the Gospel. By wagon, on horseback, on foot, and by car, they've traveled carrying the Good News of Christ from the thick forests of Virginia, across the green mountains of Kentucky, to the High Plains of Texas before finally turning back southeast to settle in sun-drenched Central Florida where three generations now pastor two churches just 20 miles apart. "

Gene has served as pastor in several Florida churches. He served in Taft (1954); Otter Creek (1954-1959); the Southside Baptist Church of Gainesville (1959-1967); the First Baptist Church of Cape Canaveral (1968-1969); and the Countryside Baptist Church, Gainesville, Florida from 1970 until his retirement in 2010.

Gene attended Stetson University, the University of Florida, and received his B.A. from Luther Rice University and Seminary.

He has many years of experience in the Christian School movement. He is the founder of the Countryside Christian School which celebrated its 40th Anniversary in 2014.

Gene also served as a Consultant and a Field Representative for Accelerated Christian Education, during which time he helped establish a number of Christian Schools in Florida. Many of his family are involved in education serving as Principals and Teachers.

Gene retired after 50 plus years in the ministry and is presently Pastor Emeritus of the Countryside Baptist Church of Gainesville, Florida. Gene turned 82 on Christmas day 2014 and spends most of his time writing and speaking.

Other Books by Gene Keith

You Can Understand The Revelation
Daniel: The Key to Prophecy
Cremation: Are You Sure?
It's All About Jesus
Religious But Lost
Suicide: Is Suicide the Unpardonable Sin?
Getting Started Right: A Handbook for Serious Christians
Easter Confusion
Evolution: Facts versus Fiction
Why do Bad Things Happen to God's People?
The Radical Same Sex Revolution
Can a Saved Person Ever be Lost Again?

Printed

If you prefer books in print, go to **CreateSpace.com** and type in Gene Keith books and you will see his books listed.

Kindle Format

If you prefer books in the Kindle format to read on IPads, IPhones and etc., simply go to **Amazon.com**, type in "Gene Keith Books," and follow the links.

You may also correspond with Gene by email: gk122532@gmail.com.

Your comments, questions, and opinions are always welcome.

Made in the USA
Charleston, SC
28 May 2015